MATH

WEEKLY
PRACTICE

Grade 3

Credits
Author: Jessica L. Snyder, M.Ed
Copy Editor: Christine Schwab, Angela Triplett

Visit *carsondellosa.com* for correlations to Common Core, state, national, and Canadian provincial standards.

Carson-Dellosa Publishing, LLC
PO Box 35665
Greensboro, NC 27425 USA
carsondellosa.com

978-1-4838-2798-8
01-053167784

Table of Contents

Introduction

The Weekly Practice series provides 40 weeks of essential daily practice in either math or language arts. It is the perfect supplement to any classroom curriculum and provides standards-based activities for every day of the week but Friday.

The activities are intended as homework assignments for Monday through Thursday and cover a wide spectrum of standards-based skills. The skills are presented at random to provide comprehensive learning but are repeated systematically throughout the book. The intention is to offer regular, focused practice to ensure mastery and retention.

Each 192-page book provides 40 weeks of reproducible pages, a standards alignment matrix, flash cards, and an answer key. The reproducible pages are perfect for homework but also work well for morning work, early finishers, and warm-up activities.

About This Book

Each page contains a variety of short, fun exercises that build in difficulty across the span of the book. The activities are divided into two sections:

- The Daily Extension Activities at the front of the book are intended to engage both student and family. These off-the-page activities are simple and fun so that students will look forward to this practice time at home. The activities span one week at a time. The instructions are clear and simple so that students can follow them with or without assistance in their homes. None need be returned to school.

- The daily practice section involves more comprehensive learning. Because of the simplicity of directions and straightforward tasks, students will be able to complete most tasks independently in a short period of time. There are four pages of activities per week, allowing for testing or a student break on Friday if desired. These pages are intended to be brought back to school.

Pages can be offered in any order, making it possible to reinforce specific skills when needed. However, skills are repeated regularly throughout the book to ensure retention over time, making a strong case for using pages sequentially.

An answer key is included for the daily practice section. You can check answers as a group for a quick follow-up lesson or monitor students' progress individually. Follow the basic page layout provided at the beginning of the answer key to match answers to page placement. Also included in the book is a set of flash cards. Reproduce them to give to students for at-home practice, or place them in classroom centers.

Common Core State Standards
Alignment Matrix

Standard	W1	W2	W3	W4	W5	W6	W7	W8	W9	W10	W11	W12	W13	W14	W15	W16	W17	W18	W19	W20
3.OA.A.1	●	●	●	●	●	●	●	●	●	●	●	●	●	●	●	●	●	●	●	●
3.OA.A.2	●		●	●	●	●	●	●	●	●	●	●	●	●	●	●	●	●	●	●
3.OA.A.3	●	●	●	●	●	●	●	●		●	●	●	●	●	●	●	●	●	●	●
3.OA.A.4	●	●	●	●	●	●	●	●	●	●	●	●	●	●	●	●	●	●	●	●
3.OA.B.5	●	●	●		●			●	●		●	●			●	●		●	●	●
3.OA.B.6		●	●	●	●	●	●	●	●	●		●	●			●	●		●	●
3.OA.C.7	●	●	●	●	●	●	●	●	●	●	●	●	●	●	●	●	●	●	●	●
3.OA.D.8	●	●	●		●	●	●	●	●	●	●	●	●	●	●	●	●		●	●
3.OA.D.9		●	●	●	●		●	●	●	●		●	●	●	●		●		●	●
3.NBT.A.1	●	●	●	●	●	●	●	●	●	●	●	●	●	●	●	●	●	●	●	●
3.NBT.A.2	●	●	●	●	●	●	●	●	●	●	●	●	●	●				●	●	
3.NBT.A.3	●	●		●	●	●	●	●		●	●	●	●		●		●	●		
3.NF.A.1	●	●	●	●	●	●	●	●		●	●		●		●	●	●	●		●
3.NF.A.2	●		●		●				●	●	●	●	●		●	●	●			
3.NF.A.3			●	●	●		●	●	●	●	●	●		●	●		●		●	●
3.MD.A.1	●	●	●	●	●		●	●	●	●	●	●	●	●	●	●		●	●	●
3.MD.A.2	●	●	●	●		●	●	●	●		●	●	●	●		●	●	●	●	●
3.MD.B.3	●		●		●			●		●			●			●			●	
3.MD.B.4	●	●	●	●	●	●	●	●		●		●	●		●		●			
3.MD.C.5	●		●		●			●	●	●		●		●	●	●		●		●
3.MD.C.6			●		●			●	●	●	●	●		●	●	●		●		●
3.MD.C.7		●		●		●	●				●		●		●		●		●	
3.MD.D.8		●	●	●	●		●	●	●			●	●		●	●		●		●
3.G.A.1	●	●		●	●			●	●	●	●	●	●	●		●	●		●	
3.G.A.2	●			●			●	●		●					●	●				●

W = Week

Common Core State Standards
Alignment Matrix

Standard	W21	W22	W23	W24	W25	W26	W27	W28	W29	W30	W31	W32	W33	W34	W35	W36	W37	W38	W39	W40
3.OA.A.1	●	●	●	●	●	●	●	●	●	●	●	●	●	●	●	●	●	●	●	●
3.OA.A.2	●	●	●	●	●	●	●	●	●	●	●	●	●	●	●	●	●	●	●	●
3.OA.A.3	●	●	●	●	●	●	●	●	●	●	●	●	●	●	●	●	●	●	●	●
3.OA.A.4	●	●	●	●	●	●	●	●	●	●	●	●	●	●	●	●	●	●	●	●
3.OA.B.5	●	●	●	●	●	●			●		●	●		●	●	●	●	●	●	●
3.OA.B.6	●	●	●	●	●	●			●		●	●				●	●	●		
3.OA.C.7	●	●	●	●	●	●	●	●	●	●	●	●	●	●	●	●	●	●	●	●
3.OA.D.8	●	●	●	●	●	●	●	●	●	●	●	●	●	●	●	●	●	●	●	●
3.OA.D.9	●		●	●	●	●	●	●	●		●	●	●	●	●	●	●			●
3.NBT.A.1	●	●	●	●	●	●	●	●	●		●	●		●	●		●	●		●
3.NBT.A.2	●	●	●	●	●	●	●	●	●	●	●	●	●	●	●	●	●	●	●	●
3.NBT.A.3	●	●	●	●	●		●		●				●	●	●					
3.NF.A.1	●			●		●	●	●	●		●	●	●		●		●	●	●	
3.NF.A.2				●		●	●		●	●		●		●	●	●	●	●	●	●
3.NF.A.3	●		●	●	●	●	●	●	●	●	●	●	●	●	●	●	●	●	●	●
3.MD.A.1	●	●	●	●	●	●	●	●	●	●		●	●	●	●	●	●	●	●	●
3.MD.A.2	●	●		●			●	●		●	●	●	●		●	●	●	●	●	●
3.MD.B.3	●						●				●		●			●	●			●
3.MD.B.4	●		●	●				●	●	●	●	●	●	●	●	●	●	●	●	
3.MD.C.5	●	●			●	●		●	●			●	●	●		●	●			●
3.MD.C.6	●	●			●	●		●	●			●	●	●		●	●			●
3.MD.C.7	●		●	●			●		●	●		●	●		●	●	●		●	●
3.MD.D.8	●	●	●	●	●	●	●		●	●	●		●	●	●	●	●	●	●	●
3.G.A.1		●			●	●		●	●		●	●	●	●	●	●	●	●	●	●
3.G.A.2				●				●					●			●			●	●

W = Week

School to Home Communication

The research is clear that family involvement is strongly linked to student success. Support for student learning at home improves student achievement in school. Educators should not underestimate the significance of this connection.

The activities in this book create an opportunity to create or improve this school-to-home link. The activities span a week at a time and can be sent home as a week-long homework packet each Monday. Simply clip together the strip of fun activities from the front of the book with the pages for Days 1 to 4 for the correct week.

Most of the activities can be completed independently, but many encourage feedback or interaction with a family member. The activities are simple and fun, aiming to create a brief pocket of learning that is enjoyable to all.

In order to make the school-to-home program work for students and their families, we encourage you to reach out to them with an introductory letter. Explain the program and its intent and ask them to partner with you in their children's educational process. Describe the role you expect them to play. Encourage them to offer suggestions or feedback along the way.

A sample letter is included below. Use it as is or create your own letter to introduce this project and elicit their collaboration.

Dear Families,

I anticipate a productive and exciting year of learning and look forward to working with you and your child. We have a lot of work to do! I hope we—teacher, student, and family—can work together as a team to achieve the goal of academic progress we all hope for this year.

I will send home a packet of homework each week on _____. There will be two items to complete each day: a single task on a strip plus a full page of focused practice. Each page or strip is labeled Day 1 (for Monday), Day 2, Day 3, or Day 4. There is no homework on Friday.

Please make sure that your student brings back the completed work _____. It is important that these are brought in on time as we may work on some of the lessons as a class.

If you have any questions about this program or would like to talk to me about it, please feel free to call or email me. Thank you for joining me in making this the best year ever for your student!

Sincerely,

_____
Name

_____
Phone

_____
Email

	Day 1	Day 2	Day 3	Day 4
Week 1	Find 20 pennies. Practice putting the pennies into different arrays. Write the number sentence for each array.	Using a deck of cards, flip over one card. Multiply the number by 10, then by 20, and finally by 30. Face cards are worth 10.	Practice telling time on the clocks in your home. If you don't have any analog clocks, you can draw your own!	Roll a pair of dice. Multiply the two numbers together. Repeat several times.
Week 2	Keep track of how many minutes you spend on homework each night this week. At the end of the week, add to find the total amount of time you spent on homework for the week.	Find a deck of cards. Remove the face cards. Aces are equal to one. Flip over six cards. Make two 3-digit numbers. Add.	A quadrilateral is a four-sided figure. How many quadrilaterals can you find around your home?	Use the produce scale at a grocery store to weigh your fruits and vegetables in ounces and pounds. Make a list.
Week 3	Practice telling multiplication and division stories at home. For example, "Mom and I share 12 crackers. How many do we each get?"	Write math facts you still need to memorize on index cards and post them around your home. Answer the fact every time you walk by.	Collect data from family or friends such as eye color or favorite sport. Use the data to create a picture graph. Don't forget the key!	Find a deck of cards. Remove the face cards. Aces are equal to one. Flip over two cards. Multiply. Write the multiplication and division fact family.
Week 4	Find a deck of cards. Remove the face cards. Aces are equal to one. Flip over three cards and make a 3-digit number. Round to the nearest 10 and 100. Repeat.	Practice skip counting by 2, 3, 4, and 5. Now try skip counting by 6, 7, 8, and 9!	Roll two dice. Draw an array with the two numbers you rolled. Write a multiplication sentence to match the array. Then, solve.	Practice telling elapsed time. For example, if you started your homework at 4:30 pm and ended at 5:00 pm, how long did you work on homework?

	Day 1	Day 2	Day 3	Day 4
Week 5	Use a ruler to practice measuring items around your home to the nearest inch and half inch.	Roll a die to create two 3-digit numbers. Create a subtraction problem. Solve.	Estimate the perimeter of your room by counting how many steps it takes to walk around its perimeter. Then, measure it. Were you close?	Practice telling time in two different ways to a family member. For example, 2:45 is "forty-five minutes after 2" and "15 minutes before 3."
Week 6	Fold a piece of paper in half. Now fold it into three equal-sized parts. You should have six equal-sized parts. Shade $\frac{5}{6}$.	Practice your sevens multiplication facts! Flip over a playing card (aces =1 and face cards = 10). Multiply that number by seven.	Using 12 counters or other small objects, create as many arrays as you can. Write the equations for each array.	If one muffin tin makes six muffins, how many muffins do three tins make? Four tins? Five tins?
Week 7	Practice turning multiplication equations into division equations. Then, practice turning division equations into multiplication equations.	Look for numbers around your neighborhood or community such as street addresses or license plates. Round each one you find to the nearest 10 or 100.	With the help of an adult, cut food such as fruit or sandwiches into fractional parts. Talk about the fractions as you eat!	What time did you get home from school today? How long will it be until dinner? Until bedtime?
Week 8	Roll a die. Multiply that number by 10, 20, 30, 40, and so on to 100. Record the multiplication equation for each.	Create and design a menu. Add prices to your food. Take orders from your family. Then, total each family member's bill.	Find a clock. What time is it? What time will it be in 1 hour? $1\frac{1}{2}$ hours? $2\frac{1}{2}$ hours?	Create your own multiplication or division tic-tac-toe boards. Make sure there are three answers in a row to win!

	Day 1	Day 2	Day 3	Day 4
Week 9	Use graph paper to draw different sizes of rectangles. Cut out and find the area by counting the squares inside.	Practice solving multiplication facts using mental math. How quickly can you remember your facts?	Use toothpicks and clay to create your own polygons such as triangles, quadrilaterals, and pentagons.	Cut out several construction paper triangles. Then, create fact family triangles. Use them as flash cards to help you memorize your multiplication facts.

	Day 1	Day 2	Day 3	Day 4
Week 10	Create multiplication problems with your friends of family. If there are three people and each person has two shoes, how many shoes are there in all?	Use number cards 1-9. Flip over one card. This is the target number. Deal five cards. Use the five numbers and any operations to make the target number.	Using a supermarket ad, circle your favorite foods. Round the prices of the items to the nearest dollar.	Estimate the length of items around your home. Use a ruler to find the exact length of the objects. How close was your estimate?

	Day 1	Day 2	Day 3	Day 4
Week 11	Write a schedule for your day. Label each activity with the time it begins. For example, 7:00 am is when you wake up, 7:15 am is when you eat breakfast, etc.	Count 18 small objects. How many different ways can you make fair shares from this group of objects? Write a division sentence for each.	Practice telling time by saying how many minutes after the hour it is and how many minutes until the next hour.	Practice writing the times tables of any multiplication facts you still need help memorizing.

	Day 1	Day 2	Day 3	Day 4
Week 12	Using playing cards 1-9, pick two cards. Draw the arrays you can make with these numbers. Write the number sentences.	Play a game outside, like basketball or tag. Give points to each action in the game. Play with a friend, and add up your points!	Use graph paper. Color rectangular arrays in the grids. Count the squares inside to find the area of each array.	Using playing cards 1-9, create two 3-digit numbers. Round each number to the nearest ten. Estimate the total.

	Day 1	Day 2	Day 3	Day 4
Week 13	Tell addition and subtraction stories while you eat. "I started with 12 green beans. I ate 4, then 2, then 3. How many are left?"	Practice writing your own number patterns. Start at any number. Then, decide what to add or subtract. Keep going!	Roll two dice. Use the numbers to write a fraction. Draw a picture to match. For example, roll a 3 and a 4 to make $\frac{3}{4}$. Draw four squares and shade three.	Your thumb is about 2 inches long. Use your thumb to estimate the length of objects at home.

	Day 1	Day 2	Day 3	Day 4
Week 14	Play "Eggs in a Basket." Roll two dice. The first number is how many baskets. The second is how many eggs in each basket. Draw and solve.	Look for arrays, such as quilt patterns, in the real world. Record at least five of your findings.	Find the height, in inches, of friends and/or family members. Who is tallest? How much taller? Who is shorter? How much shorter?	With the help of an adult, research the cost of airplane tickets. Pick a destination and try to find the least expensive ticket price.

	Day 1	Day 2	Day 3	Day 4
Week 15	Ounces measure the mass, or weight, of small objects. Find some items at home that you would measure in ounces.	Roll two dice. Multiply the numbers. Write all the possible multiplication and division sentences using the two numbers.	Look for large numbers at home. Practice reading the numbers. Round the numbers to the nearest hundred.	Make up your own division stories using fair shares. For example, "32 stickers shared evenly with 4 friends is 8 stickers per friend."

	Day 1	Day 2	Day 3	Day 4
Week 16	Count 24 small objects from around your home. Think of all the different ways you can share them equally.	Find a deck of cards and a partner. Remove the face cards. Flip two and multiply. The greatest product wins the round!	A right angle is 90° and is shaped like an "L." Can you find right angles around your home?	Practice memorizing your multiplication facts. Roll one die. Write the multiplication table for that number.

	Day 1	Day 2	Day 3	Day 4
Week 17	Look for polygons around your neighborhood. Can you find any octagons? Pentagons? Trapezoids? Make a list.	Make up multiplication stories in the kitchen. For example, three bowls with eight blueberries in each bowl is 24 blueberries.	What time is it now? What time was it $2\frac{1}{2}$ hours ago? What time will it be $3\frac{1}{2}$ hours from now? $4\frac{1}{2}$ hours?	Look for containers in your home that hold more than, less than, or about one liter of a liquid.

	Day 1	Day 2	Day 3	Day 4
Week 18	Using playing cards 1-9, flip over three cards. Make one 3-digit number. About how many hundreds are in it?	Roll one die. Make two 3-digit numbers. Subtract. Remember to subtract the smaller number from the larger!	Look for objects around your home that you would measure in grams. How about objects you would measure in kilograms?	Ask your parents if you can collect recyclables at home. Total how many recyclable items you collect in one week.

	Day 1	Day 2	Day 3	Day 4
Week 19	A classroom has 24 desks. How many ways can you arrange the desks into rows with the same number of desks in each row?	A dozen equals 12. A half dozen equals six. How many half dozens do you need to make 12? 24? 36?	Flip two number cards 1-9 to make a 2-digit number. How many equal groups can you make out of this number?	Bottles of soda are sold in 1- or 2-liter bottles. Find an empty soda bottle and fill it with water. Pour it into a quart bottle to see the difference in volumes. Which holds the most?

	Day 1	Day 2	Day 3	Day 4
Week 20	Do some math at the dinner table! An example would be four people sitting at the table. Each person has two tacos. How many tacos do they have in all?	Bake cookies with an adult. How many cookies can you fit on one tray? Based on your answer, how many trays would you need to make 36 cookies? 48 cookies?	The next time you help carry in the groceries, think of math! If there are 12 items in a bag and you carry in 4 bags, how many items did you carry in all?	Look for a sheet of stickers at home or in a store. How many stickers are on the sheet? How many would be on two sheets? three sheets? 10 sheets?

	Day 1	Day 2	Day 3	Day 4
Week 21	What time did you eat breakfast today? When did you eat lunch? How long did you go between breakfast and lunch?	Create and solve elapsed time problems based on your evening and bedtime schedule.	Help fold your family's laundry. Fold the clothes into equal piles. Create and solve a multiplication problem.	Cut pieces of yarn or string found at home. Measure each piece with a ruler to the nearest $\frac{1}{4}$ and $\frac{1}{2}$ inch.
Week 22	A hexagon is a six-sided figure. Find and record any hexagons you notice in your home.	Ask an adult to help you make your own trail mix. Divide the mix into equal amounts of each ingredient per batch.	Roll two dice. The second number is how many times you will multiply the first number. Write the multiplication sentence. Then, write a repeated addition fact to match.	Look in your own backyard for math problems! Look for groups or arrays of items such as plants, birds in trees, flower gardens, etc.
Week 23	Use a ruler to measure the lengths of a book. Round to the nearest inch. Find the area and perimeter of the book's cover.	Do you still have facts you need to memorize? Write them on index cards and use them as flash cards to practice your facts.	Flip two number cards, 1–9. Make a 2-digit number. Write a multiplication and division fact family using the two numbers. Hint: One times any number is that number!	How many glasses of water do you drink each day? Keep track of your totals and tally at the end of the week.
Week 24	Create your own elapsed time problems using train or bus schedules.	Use books or the Internet to research the mass of different coins.	Draw a blank number line. Label it from 0 to 1. Practice plotting and labeling different fractions such as $\frac{1}{2}$, $\frac{1}{4}$, and so on.	Roll one die. Draw a square and divide it into equal-sized pieces according to the number you rolled.

	Day 1	Day 2	Day 3	Day 4
Week 25	Look for parallel lines at home and in your neighborhood. List them or their locations.	Count any money you may have saved. What could you buy with this amount? How much more do you need to buy something you really want?	Make up math problems that involve sharing food. Use what you have in the kitchen and make fair shares with someone.	Ask an adult for some toothpicks. How many triangles can you make with three toothpicks? Six toothpicks? Nine toothpicks? Thirty toothpicks?

	Day 1	Day 2	Day 3	Day 4
Week 26	Arrange similar objects in your bedroom, such as toys, socks, or shoes, into different arrays. Write the multiplication sentence.	Draw a circle. Cut it into fourths. How many fourths make one whole? Repeat with another circle. Try thirds and sixths.	With the help of an adult, use a ruler to measure the lengths of a window in your home. Find the perimeter.	Look for different polygons around your home. Count how many pairs of parallel sides each polygon has.

	Day 1	Day 2	Day 3	Day 4
Week 27	Roll dice to get six numbers. Draw an irregular shape with those numbers as measurements. Find the perimeter.	Use the newspaper or Internet to find movie times. Create elapsed time problems to solve.	Count how many fiction and nonfiction books you have at home. Estimate the difference and then subtract.	Create number riddles such as: I am thinking of a number that is between 40 and 50, can be divided by six, and has a two in the ones place.

	Day 1	Day 2	Day 3	Day 4
Week 28	Practice solving elapsed time problems using a number line. "Hop" the hours down the line first, then the minutes!	Think of little jobs you can do around the house, or even in your neighborhood. What would be a fair amount of money to charge for each job? How much could you earn in all?	Roll two dice. Write the multiplication fact. Use the commutative property to write the "turn-around" fact. For example, $3 \times 4 = 4 \times 3$.	Create your own polygon riddles! An example could be: I am a polygon with four equal sides. Who am I?

	Day 1	Day 2	Day 3	Day 4
Week 29	A square is a special rectangle. Is a rectangle a square? Is a rhombus a square or a rectangle? Prove it.	Roll two dice. Use the numbers to write a fraction. Draw the fraction.	Pick an item you would like to save money for. How much money do you have now? How much more do you need?	Find a group of small objects. Make fraction problems. For example, eight snacks may total: $\frac{3}{8}$ pretzels plus $\frac{5}{8}$ crackers.
Week 30	Use a ruler to measure the lengths of 10 crayons to the nearest quarter inch. Plot the data on a line plot.	Help pack lunches for you and your family. How many sandwiches did you pack in all? How many pieces of bread? Fruits?	Look around your home for items that come in packs, such as crayons. If the crayons come in packs of 24, how many crayons are in two packs?	Roll two dice twice. Use the four numbers to make two fractions. Create a drawing to help you compare the fractions. Use the appropriate symbol: **>, <,** or **=**.
Week 31	How many people are in your family? How many boys? How many girls? Write a fraction for each.	Draw a giant inch! Use a ruler to draw a 6-inch line. Label it from 0 to 1. At what spot would you label $\frac{1}{2}$ inch? $\frac{1}{4}$? $\frac{3}{4}$?	What time did you go to bed last night? What time did you wake up this morning? How long did you sleep?	Count the clocks in your home. How many of them are digital? How many are analog? Write a fraction for each type of clock.
Week 32	Use a ruler to measure the lengths of your family's shoes. Create a line plot with the data.	Roll a die. Draw that number of circles. Roll again. Split each circle into that many pieces. How many pieces in all?	Go for a walk with your family. If each person walked two miles, how many total miles did your family walk in all?	Look in your refrigerator and food cupboard. Which items could you measure in milliliters? Liters? Grams? Kilograms?

	Day 1	Day 2	Day 3	Day 4
Week 33	Make number cards from 1 to 10. Flip over the top card. Multiply that number by your age. Repeat with other family members' ages.	Review place value. Flip five cards to make a 5-digit number. Repeat. Compare the two numbers with >, <, or =.	Find 10 objects in nature. Measure them to the nearest $\frac{1}{2}$ inch. Plot the data on a line plot.	Use sidewalk chalk to draw a maze of multiplication problems. Follow the even products from start to finish!

	Day 1	Day 2	Day 3	Day 4
Week 34	Write multiplication facts on index cards. Play catch with a partner. Every time the ball drops, pick a card and say the fact!	Find a partner and a deck of cards. Flip over two cards (face cards = 10, aces =1). Multiply the two numbers. The first person to correctly shout out the answer wins the cards!	Find the birthdays of 10 people. Create a bar graph and line plot to order their birthdays. Which is an easier way to look at the data?	Flip over two cards (face cards = 10, aces = 1). Use the numbers to draw a rectangle. Find the area. Find the perimeter.

	Day 1	Day 2	Day 3	Day 4
Week 35	Look for and record any perpendicular lines you can find around your home. Do you see the right angles?	Roll dice to create two 3-digit numbers. The first number is one addend of an addition problem. The second number is the sum. Find the missing addend!	Look for trapezoids around your home and community. Draw them and trace the parallel lines.	Flip over two number cards from a stack, 1-9. Write a multiplication sentence. Draw a picture to match. What other math sentences can you make with these numbers?

	Day 1	Day 2	Day 3	Day 4
Week 36	Collect 10 leaves and measure them to the nearest $\frac{1}{4}$ inch. Create a line plot with your data.	Imagine you are making cookies for a bake sale. How many cookies would you want to make? How many batches? How many in each batch?	Flip over two number cards from a stack, 1-9. Create a fraction with the two numbers. Is this fraction > or < $\frac{1}{2}$?	Roll three dice. Write a multiplication sentence. Use the distributive property to solve.

	Day 1	Day 2	Day 3	Day 4
Week 37	Create your own picture graph. Choose what type of data you want to collect and how you want to represent it.	Roll dice to make two three-digit numbers. Round each number to the nearest ten, and subtract.	Flip over a number card from a stack, 1-9. Write the "times table" for that number. Highlight any facts you haven't memorized yet.	Roll two dice. Draw a rectangle with those numbers as the side lengths. Find the area of the rectangle.
Week 38	Flip over two playing cards (face cards = 10, aces = 1). The first number tells how many squares to draw. The second number tells how many circles to draw in each square. Follow the directions.	Write your own division problems with facts you know. Act out the problems for a friend or family member.	Roll one die. Draw a number line and split it into that many parts. Label the endpoints 0 and 1. Label each fraction on the number line.	Use a pitcher at home to measure one liter of water. How many drinking glasses can you fill with the water?
Week 39	Look for fences around your community. Estimate the lengths of the sides to find the area or perimeter. Hint: An adult's foot is a little less than one foot!	Make pizzas at home. How many slices can you cut from the whole? What fraction of the pizza did you eat?	Flip over two number cards 1-9. Make a fraction with the two numbers. Write two fractions that are less, and two that are greater.	Build a tower with blocks. How many blocks did you use in one tower? How many blocks did you need for two towers? For three towers?
Week 40	Flip over two number cards from a stack, 1-9. Multiply them. Write a story to match. Divide them. Write a story to match.	Collect data on the color preferences of family members. Make your own bar graph at home! Don't forget the title and labels.	Roll one die. Use that number to create your own rule table. Choose the operation and starting numbers.	Roll two dice. Multiply the numbers on top. Draw a shape using that number as the perimeter. Choose the unit. Find the area.

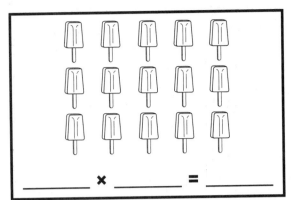

_____ × _____ = _____

326

Round to the nearest

10 = _____

Round to the nearest

100 = _____

---

100 − 58 = _____

_____ : _____

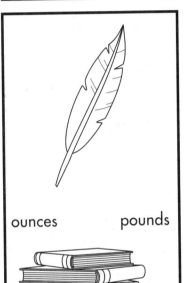

ounces   pounds

ounces   pounds

I am a quadrilateral with four equal sides. What shape am I?

_____

Draw me.

Each softball team has 9 players. There are 72 players in all. How many teams are there?

---

349 + 567 = _____

How many legs are on

2 horses? _____

3 horses? _____

4 horses? _____

Student's Pets

dogs	🙂 🙂 🙂 🙂 🙂
cats	🙂 🙂
fish	🙂 🙂 🙂

🙂 = 2 students

How many students have dogs? _____

How many students have cats? _____

How many more students have fish than cats? _____

Name _____

Make the equations true.

$3 \times$ 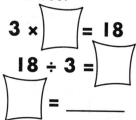 $= 18$

$18 \div 3 =$ ⬚

⬚ $=$ _____

Mr. Sherman drove 234 miles in week one. In week two, he drove 148 miles. In week three, he drove 287 miles. How many more miles did he drive in weeks one and two than he did in week three?

$2 \times 10 = 20$

$2 \times 20 =$ _____

$2 \times 30 =$ _____

$2 \times 40 =$ _____

$2 \times 50 =$ _____

$2 \times 60 =$ _____

$2 \times 70 =$ _____

Color $\frac{3}{4}$ of the rectangle.

Which is greater?

$200 + 30 + 2$

$200 + 40 + 1$

$\begin{array}{r} 905 \\ - 678 \\ \hline \end{array}$

Count the tiles to find the area of the square.

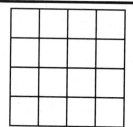

area = _____ **square units**

A movie starts at 1:00 pm and ends at 3:15 pm. How long is the movie?

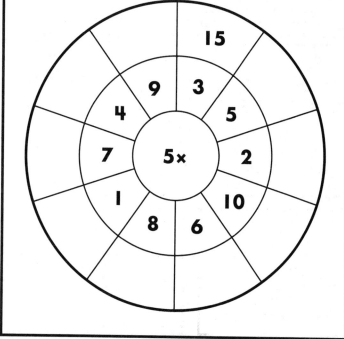

Place each number on the number line. Then, round to the nearest 10.
A. 13 _____   B. 18 _____
C. 11 _____   D. 15 _____

○ **4:40**

○ **8:40**

○ **8:20**

○ **4:20**

Draw lines to break the rhombus into fourths. Label each fourth.

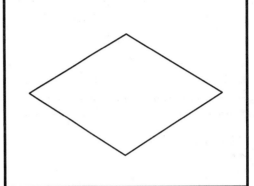

Solve the problems. Use the key to color in the flag.

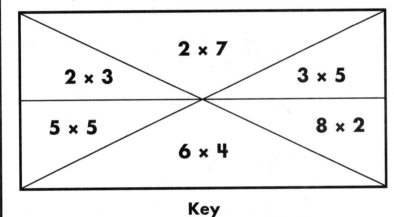

2 × 7

2 × 3

3 × 5

5 × 5

8 × 2

6 × 4

Key
4 in the ones place: blue
5 in the ones place: red
6 in the ones place: green

556 + 378 = _____

Write >, <, or =.

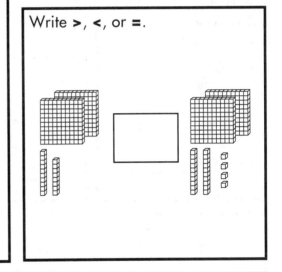

Complete the fact family.

4 × 8 = _____

8 × 4 = _____

_____ ÷ 4 = 8

_____ ÷ 8 = 4

_____

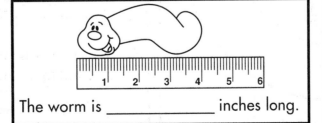

The worm is _____ inches long.

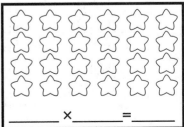

_____ × _____ = _____

About how much does a puppy weigh?

○ **10 ounces**

○ **10 pounds**

○ **10 inches**

Finish labeling the number line.

7,459

Round to nearest

10: _____

100: _____

Coral has 60 cents in her pocket. She has 4 coins. What coins does she have? Draw a picture to solve.

_____ _____ _____ _____

Jacob had $45 saved. He spent $12 at the movie theater. How much money did he have left?

498 is about _____.

$$7 \times \boxed{} = 21$$

$$\boxed{} = \_\_\_\_\_$$

Draw an array to solve:

$$8 \times 6 = \_\_\_\_\_$$

H	T	O
9	0	5
− 6	7	8

Ben is 9 years old. His sister Aimee is 4 years older than him. He is 2 years older than his brother Trey. How old are Aimee and Trey?

James raked the leaves in his backyard. His mom paid him $2.00 for each bag of leaves he filled. On Saturday, he filled 6 bags. On Sunday, he filled 5 bags. How much money did he make in all?

What division problem could be solved with this array?

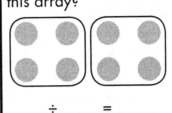

_____ ÷ _____ = _____

$32 \div 4 =$ _____

3:48

Measure to the nearest half inch.

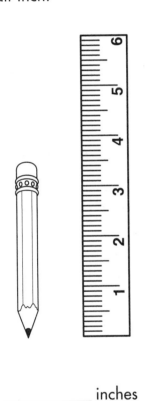

_____ inches

Find at least three ways to get to 20. You may go up, down, left to right, and diagonally. Use **+**, **–**, and **×**.

2	3	6	8
4	5	3	7
2	9	8	5

4 tens + 6 ones

3 tens + 3 ones

782 – 597 = _____

Draw an array for 3 × 5.

Draw four different quadrilaterals.

○ **336**
○ **363**
○ **633**

What fraction of the hats are gray?

What fraction of the hats are white?

twenty-five after 7

$18 \div \square = 3$

$\square = $ _____

$\begin{array}{r} 1000 \\ -\ 846 \\ \hline \end{array}$

Multiply length by width to find the area.

4 units

2 units

area = _____ sq. units

Think of four ways to write 24.

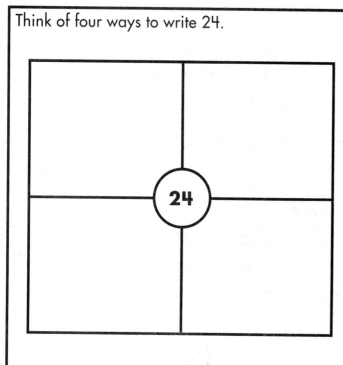

623, ____ , 643, ____ , 663, ____

100	
23	

For homework, Michelle reads 20 minutes on Monday, 23 minutes on Tuesday, 34 minutes on Wednesday, and 29 minutes on Thursday. Her goal was to read 100 minutes over the four days. Did she reach her goal? How do you know?

Soccer practice started at 5:30 pm. The clock shows what time practice finished. How long was practice?

_____

Add to find the perimeter.

5 in.

2 in.   2 in.

5 in.

perimeter = _____ in.

$14 \div \boxed{} = 2$ $\boxed{} = $ ___

Color to show $\frac{3}{6}$.

Henry had 36 trading cards. He divided them equally into 4 groups. How many cards were in each group?

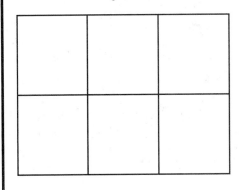

___ × ___ = ___

981
Round to nearest

10: _____

100: _____

494
+ 356

- ○ **about 1 liter**
- ○ **more than 1 liter**
- ○ **less than 1 liter**

The pet store had puppies for sale. There were 4 baskets with 3 puppies in each basket. How many puppies were there?

_____ × _____ = _____

☐ **times 5 equals 45**

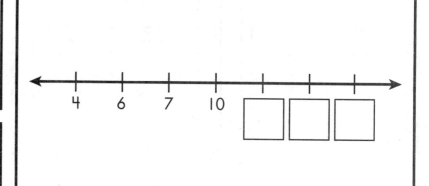

4   6   7   10   ☐ ☐ ☐

Students' Favorite Sports

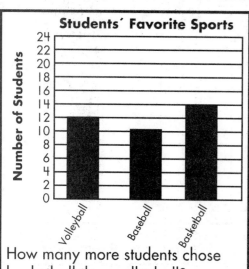

How many more students chose basketball than volleyball? _____

How many fewer students chose baseball than basketball? _____

$63 ÷ 9 =$ ☐

$$\begin{array}{r} 40 \\ \times\ 7 \\ \hline \end{array}$$

---

7 × 0 = _____

7 × 1 = _____

7 × 2 = _____

7 × 3 = _____

7 × 4 = _____

7 × 5 = _____

7 × 6 = _____

7 × 7 = _____

7 × 8 = _____

7 × 9 = _____

7 × 10 = _____

Tool to weigh objects:

- ○ **ruler**
- ○ **scale**
- ○ **measuring cup**

Write **>**, **<**, or **=**.

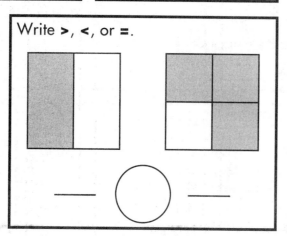

_____ ◯ _____

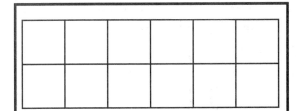

area = _____ square units

**10 tens and
5 more =**

398 + 389 = _____

Divide the rectangle into
4 equal parts. Label
each part.

× 4	
2	**8**
7	
4	
6	
9	
8	
5	

Write a math story to match the
expression **24 ÷ 3**.

_____

_____

_____

_____

_____

_____

_____

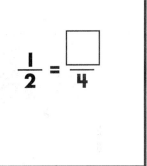

$\frac{1}{2} = \frac{\square}{4}$

8 × 8 = _____

7 × 4 = ⬜

⬜ ÷ 4 = ⬜

Martez collects baseball cards. He has 48 in his collection. He
buys 2 packs of 8 cards. Then, he gives his brother 2 cards. How
many baseball cards does he have now? Show your work in the
space below.

Plot the fractions on the number line: $\frac{1}{4}$, $\frac{1}{2}$, $\frac{3}{4}$.

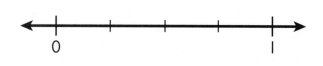

0   1

× 6	
4	24
5	
3	
8	
7	
6	
10	

Draw a line to match.

49 ÷ 7	2
18 ÷ 9	3
36 ÷ 6	7
20 ÷ 5	4
24 ÷ 3	5
24 ÷ 8	6
35 ÷ 7	8

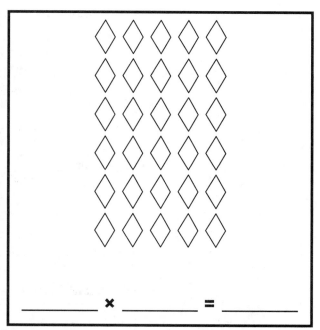

_____ × _____ = _____

Aja awoke at 7:05 am and was ready for school at 7:50 am. How long did it take her to get ready for school?

_____

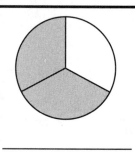

_____

8
18

39

502, _____, 522, _____, _____

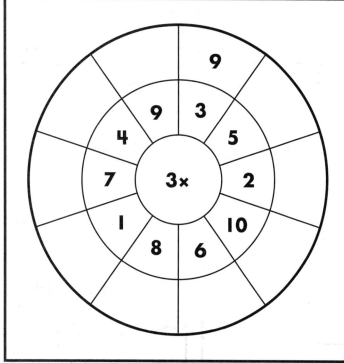

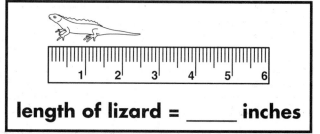

length of lizard = _____ inches

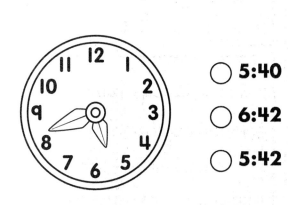

○ 5:40

○ 6:42

○ 5:42

Five friends shared 40 jellybeans. How many jellybeans did each friend get?

Students' Hair Color

Brown	♀ ♀ ♀ ♀ ♀ ♀ ♀
Black	♀ ♀ ♀ ♀ ♀
Blonde	♀ ♀ ♀ ♀ ♀ ᛃ
Red	♀ ᛃ

♀ = 2 students

How many students have brown hair color? _____
How many students have red hair color? _____
How many more students have blonde hair than black hair? _____

432 rounded to the nearest 10 = _____

Estimate to find the difference.

784
− 123   **is about**   ☐
                        − ☐

9 × 0	
9 × 1	
9 × 2	
9 × 3	
9 × 4	
9 × 5	
9 × 6	
9 × 7	
9 × 8	
9 × 9	
9 × 10	

Complete the pattern.

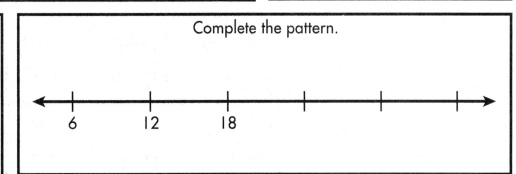

6   12   18

perimeter = _____ ft.

6 ft.
3 ft.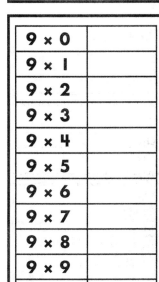

If ☐ x 7 = 56,

then ☐ ÷ 7 = ☐.

Divide into sixths. Label each part.

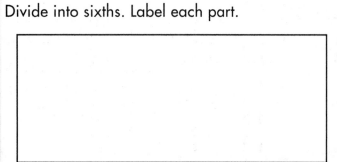

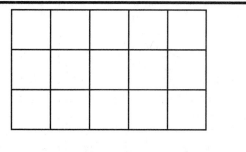

area = _____ **square units**

If **32 ÷ 8 =** ▢ ,

then ▢ **× 8 = 32.**

▢ **= _____**

Juan's basketball practice starts at 4:15 pm and ends at 5:45 pm. How long is practice? Use the number line.

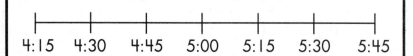

4:15   4:30   4:45   5:00   5:15   5:30   5:45

Juan's practice is _____ long.

Sidney read one 203-page book, and one 159-page book. Her brother Sam read one book that was 360 pages long. Who read more pages?

36 ÷ 6 = _____

5 × 6 = ___ × ___

Draw a line to match.

3 × 4	**30**
6 × 2	**14**
7 × 3	**12**
6 × 3	**24**
5 × 4	**12**
7 × 2	**20**
8 × 3	**21**
5 × 6	**18**

9 × 7 = _____

_____ × 9 = 63

63 ÷ _____ = 9

_____ ÷ 9 = 7

About how much does a loaf of bread weigh?

◯ **one pound**

◯ **one ounce**

◯ **one gram**

Edie bought a bag of pears at the market that weighed 31 ounces. Jayson bought a bag of peaches that weighed 16 ounces. How many total ounces of fruit did Edie and Jayson buy?

O O O O O O

O O O O O O

O O O O O O

____ × ____ = ____

347 + 478 = ____

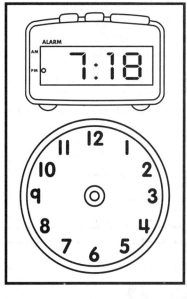

× 8	
4	
8	
7	
9	
5	
6	
3	

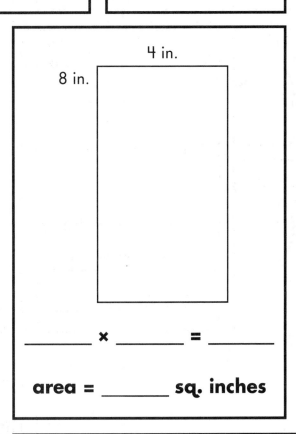

4 in.

8 in.

____ × ____ = ____

area = _____ sq. inches

653
− 278

+ 278

9 × 7 = _____

197	
	23

Plot 326 on the number line. Answer the questions to round to the nearest hundred.

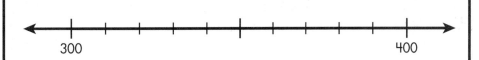

300   400

326 is between _____ and _____.

326 is closer to _____ than _____.

326 rounded to the nearest hundred is _____.

Sophia had two baskets with 8 books in each basket. She let a friend borrow 2 books. How many books did she have left?

+ 12	
12	
24	36
36	
48	
60	
72	

Write a division equation to match the model.

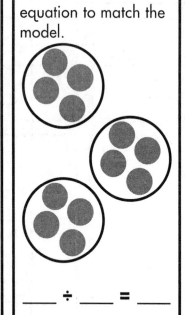

____ ÷ ____ = ____

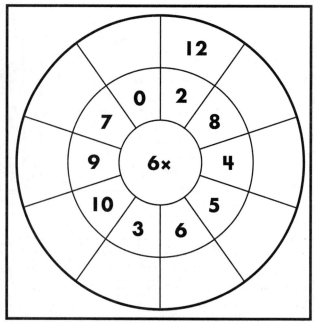

$\square \times 9 = 36$

$36 \div 9 = \square$

$\square = \underline{\quad}$

Shade in $\frac{3}{4}$.

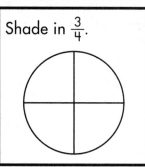

$3 \times 1 = \underline{\qquad}$

$3 \times 10 = \underline{\qquad}$

$3 \times 20 = \underline{\qquad}$

$3 \times 30 = \underline{\qquad}$

725, ____, 775, ____, 825, ____

Solve. Use the key to color in each section.

20 ÷ 2	16 ÷ 4
6 × 2	36 ÷ 6

Key
4 in the ones place: blue
2 in the ones place: green
6 in the ones place: purple
0 in the ones place: yellow

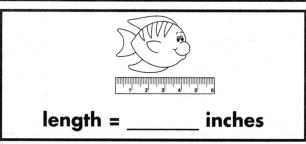

length = _____ inches

$$\frac{2}{4} \; \square \; \frac{3}{4}$$

○ >

○ <

○ =

954

Round to nearest

10: _____

100: _____

The Johnston family started driving to their family reunion. The reunion was 985 miles away from home. They drove 446 miles on Saturday and 423 miles on Sunday. How many more miles do they need to drive to get to their destination?

$35 \div 7 = \boxed{}$, so $\boxed{} \times 7 = 35$.

$\boxed{} \times 8 = 48$

$8 \times \boxed{} = 48$

$\boxed{} = \underline{}$

	× 5
2	
3	
4	
5	
6	
7	
8	
9	
10	

Complete the bar model to solve 30 ÷ 5.

30				
6				

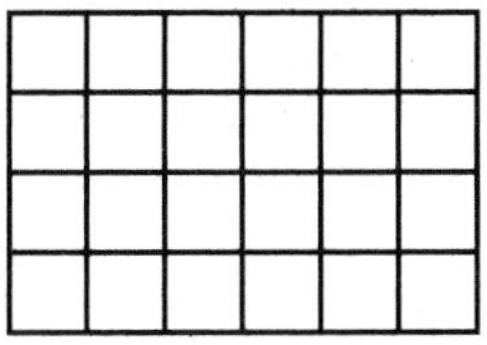

area = _____ square units

900
− 485

Find the perimeter.

6 cm.

perimeter = _____ cm

Danny has 14 pieces of gum. He shares the gum equally with his sister. How many pieces of gum do they each get? Write a division equation to solve.

_____ ÷ _____ = _____

Estimate to the nearest hundred.

987 is about _____.

Circle the quadrilaterals.

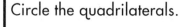

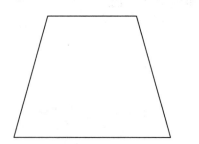

What is the name of this shape?

_____

How many angles does this shape have? _____

81 ÷ 9 = _____

$\frac{3}{3}$ = _____ **whole**

Jaime´s dance class started at 6:00 pm. It lasted 1 hour and 10 minutes. Draw the time her dance class was over.

```
H|T|O
8|0|6
-5|6|7
```

Write >, <, or =.

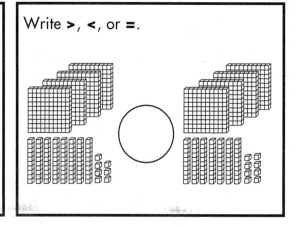

Meg has 5 coins in her pocket that total 46¢. Which coins does she have?

$\frac{5}{10}$ ◯ $\frac{1}{2}$

$8 \times \boxed{} = 64$

_____ minutes to 4

_____ minutes past 3

× 3	
0	
1	
2	
3	
4	
5	
6	
7	
8	

I am a polygon with 8 sides, and 8 angles. Who am I? _____
Draw me. Label my sides and angles.

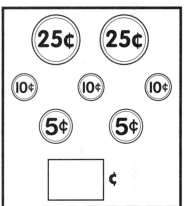

⬜ ¢

$507 - 237 =$ _____

$45 \div \boxed{} = 9$

$\boxed{} \times 9 = 45$

$\boxed{} =$ _____

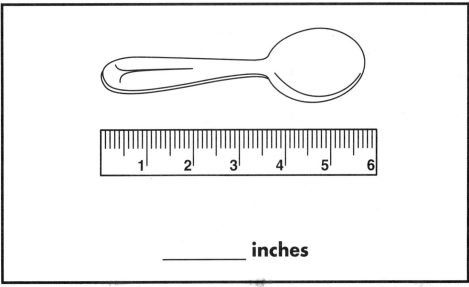

_____ **inches**

800
− 489

○ 310

○ 311

○ 321

÷ 2	
4	
8	
12	
16	
20	
10	

Draw an array to show 4 × 7 = 28.

$5\overline{)40}$

____ × 4 = 24

4 × 6 = ____

____ ÷ 6 = 4

24 ÷ ____ = 6

A flight left the airport at 2:35 pm. It landed at 5:05 pm. How long was the flight?

_____, 126, _____, _____, 156

4 × 2 × 5 = (4 × 2) × 5

true   false

Circle the fractions that show $\frac{2}{3}$.

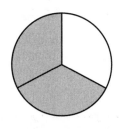

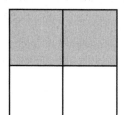

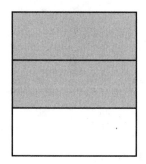

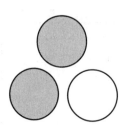

Four friends shared 32 counters equally. How many counters did each friend get? Draw a picture and write an equation to show your work.

7,487
Rounded to the nearest

ten : _____

hundred: _____

4,091
Rounded to the nearest

ten : _____

hundred: _____

If $27 \div 3 = 9$, then

_____ ÷ _____ = _____.

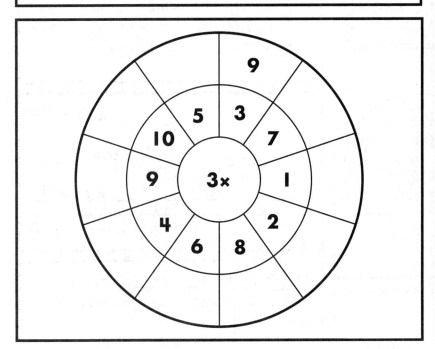

Find the area.

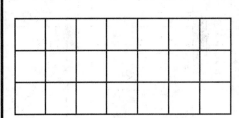

A = _____ square units

Draw a line to match.

6 × 4   28

4 × 3   15

2 × 7   24

7 × 4   18

3 × 5   12

6 × 3   14

Plot the fractions on the number line.

$A = \frac{1}{3}$ $B = \frac{2}{3}$ $C = \frac{3}{3}$

←———————|————————|————————|————————→

A rectangle has two sides that are 6 cm long and two sides that are 3 cm long. What is the perimeter?

_____ cm

---

4 × 10 = _____

4 × 20 = _____

4 × 30 = _____

Jasper walked home from school. He walked about:

○ **1 yard**

○ **1 foot**

○ **1 mile**

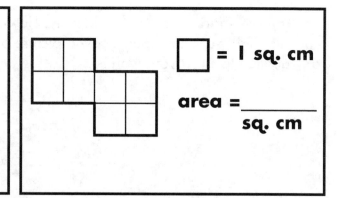

= 1 sq. cm

area = _____
sq. cm

904 – 276 = _____

Kali scored 2 goals in her soccer game on Saturday. In Monday's game, she scored 1 less than she scored on Saturday. In Thursday's game, she scored 1 goal. How many goals did she score in all three games?

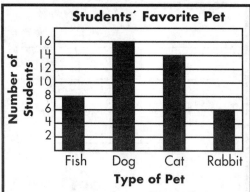

Students' Favorite Pet

How many students chose fish?

_____

How many more students chose dogs than cats? _____

How many fewer students chose rabbits than fish? _____

_____ **× 4 = 36**

9 × _____ **= 54**

_____ **=** _____

÷ 4	
4	
8	
12	
16	
20	
24	

Mr. Ortiz packed 3 sandwich bags with 8 pretzels in each bag. How many pretzels did he pack in all?

_____ : _____

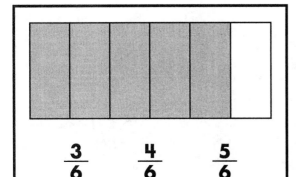

$$\frac{3}{6} \qquad \frac{4}{6} \qquad \frac{5}{6}$$

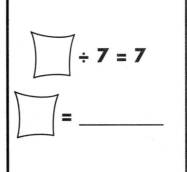

$$\square \div 7 = 7$$

$$\square = \underline{\qquad}$$

754 + 136 = _____

Charlie read three books with 70 pages each. How many pages did he read? Write a number sentence. Solve the problem.

8 × 0	
8 × 1	
8 × 2	
8 × 3	
8 × 4	
8 × 5	
8 × 6	
8 × 7	
8 × 8	
8 × 9	
8 × 10	

Sherri has 28 flowers. She gives 4 flowers to her sister. She puts the remaining flowers in vases, with 6 in each vase. If she puts an equal number of flowers in each vase, how many vases does she need?

Serena had 6 friends at her sleepover party. She gave each friend 2 cookies. How many cookies did she share?

6)42

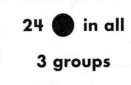

24 ● in all

3 groups

_____ ● in each group

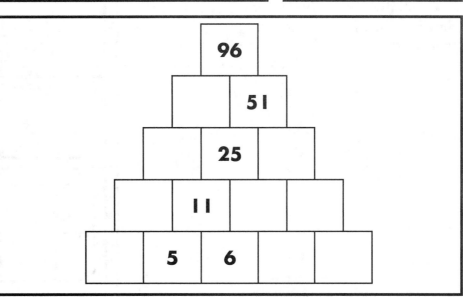

Write >, <, or =.

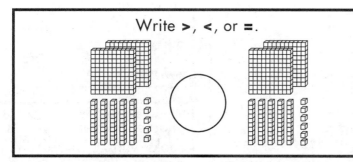

$\bigcirc$

7 × 0	
7 × 1	
7 × 2	
7 × 3	
7 × 4	
7 × 5	
7 × 6	
7 × 7	
7 × 8	
7 × 9	
7 × 10	

÷ 7	
35	
14	
42	
70	
56	
21	
49	
63	
7	
28	

Kyle and his dad went for a bike ride. They rode for 20 minutes, then played catch at the park for 30 minutes. They rode 20 minutes back home. They left their house at 9:00 am. What time did they get home?

_____ minutes after _____

$$\begin{array}{r} 70 \\ \times\ 5 \\ \hline \end{array}$$

$10\overline{)60}$

$$\begin{array}{r} 224 \\ +388 \\ \hline \end{array}$$

is about

$\boxed{}$
+ $\boxed{}$

8 × _____ = 72

236	
78	

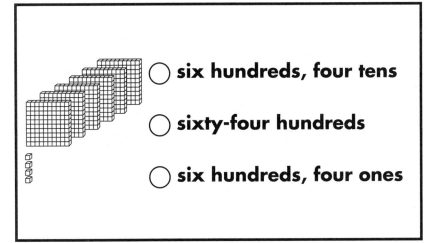

○ **six hundreds, four tens**

○ **sixty-four hundreds**

○ **six hundreds, four ones**

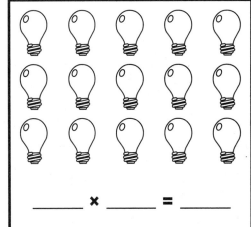

_____ × _____ = _____

Heidi played 4 games at the carnival. She won 2 small prizes at each game. How many prizes did she win altogether? Draw a picture and write an equation to solve.

103 is about _____.

☐ × ☐ = 36

36 ÷ ☐ = ☐

☐ = _____

36 ÷ 9	8
54 ÷ 9	9
81 ÷ 9	5
27 ÷ 9	4
45 ÷ 9	3
72 ÷ 9	6

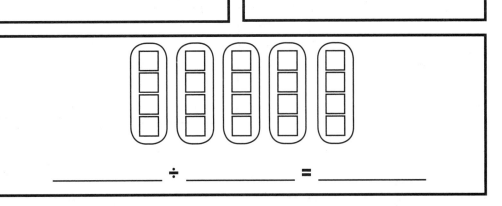

_____ ÷ _____ = _____

If 3 × ☐ = 24,

then 24 ÷ 8 = ☐ .

600
− 492
_____

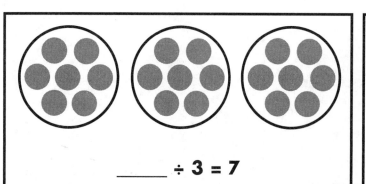

_____ ÷ 3 = 7

Kristi made 2 tins of 6 muffins. How many muffins did she make in all?

_____ × _____ = _____

64 ÷ _____ = 8

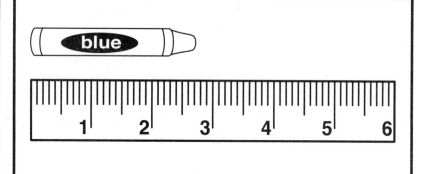

_____ = inches

499 + 499 = _____

37 minutes after 4

2 × ☐ = 18

18 ÷ 2 = ☐

Rule: × 3	
5	
8	
6	
3	
4	
2	
7	
9	
1	
10	

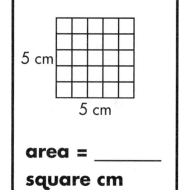

5 cm

5 cm

area = _____
square cm

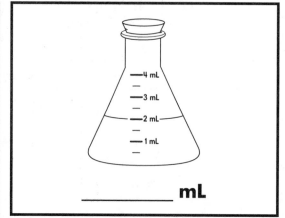

_____ mL

Multiply to find the area.

8 cm

4 cm

area = _____ sq. cm

How many 4s are in 12? _____

_____ × 6 = 54

Rule: ×5	
2	10
3	15
4	20
5	
6	
7	

---

10 ÷ 1	
9 ÷ 1	
8 ÷ 1	
7 ÷ 1	
6 ÷ 1	
5 ÷ 1	
4 ÷ 1	
3 ÷ 1	
2 ÷ 1	
1 ÷ 1	

Solve. Circle the three problems in a row that have the same answer.

2 × 7	4 × 6	4 × 5
3 × 3	3 × 8	4 × 8
5 × 6	6 × 4	7 × 4

Draw a picture.

36 ÷ 9 = _____

---

804 – 159 = _____

Jayla had 29 marbles. Kaia had 18 marbles. About how many more marbles did Jayla have than Kaia?

Liam wants to buy a remote control car that costs $35. He has $12 saved. His mother gave him $4 for mowing the lawn, but he gave $2 to his brother for helping. Show your work.

How much money does he have now? _____

How much more money does he need to buy the car? _____

532	
	166

Kevin's basketball team scored 52 points. The opposing team scored 47 points. About how many points total were scored during the game?

about _____ points

perimeter =

_____ inches

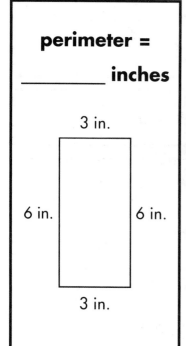

3 in.

6 in.   6 in.

3 in.

÷ 4	
32	
12	
40	
28	
36	
8	
4	
16	
20	
24	

4 × 30

5 × 40

6 × 50

700
− 548

There are 124 third graders at Westville Elementary. There are 147 fourth-graders, and 112 fifth-graders. How many students are there in all three grades combined?

Jackson starts watching a movie at 7:10 pm. The clock shows the time the movie ended. How long was the movie?

20 ÷ 5 = ☐

What fraction of the triangles are shaded?

_____

Makenzie counted 8 dogs at the dog park. Then, 2 more dogs came. After a half hour, 4 dogs left. How many dogs were left?

There were _____ dogs left.

_____ : _____

Color the ants to match each fraction.

$\frac{2}{6}$ $\frac{1}{4}$ $\frac{1}{2}$

45 ÷ 5 = ____

How many wheels on:

1 tricycle? _____

2 tricycles? _____

3 tricycles? _____

4 tricycles? _____

Draw a line to match.

32	**4 × 3**
16	**4 × 7**
12	**4 × 5**
24	**4 × 8**
28	**4 × 4**
20	**4 × 6**

Write **>**, **<**, or **=**.

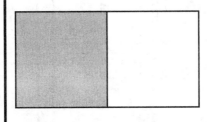   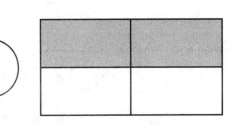

Each table at the restaurant can seat 8 people. A party of 24 people came to eat. How many tables will they need?

One paper clip weighs 100 grams.

true   false

Reilly got home from school at 3:15 pm. She ate a snack and played with her sister for 30 minutes, then she did homework for 40 minutes. At what time did she finish her homework?

○ **4:15**   ○ **4:20**   ○ **4:25**

Zach has 4 bins of action figures. Each bin holds 8 figures. How many action figures does he have?

_____ × _____ = _____

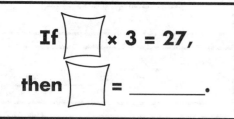

If ⬚ × 3 = 27,

then ⬚ = _____ .

Ashton grew tomato plants in his backyard. Each tomato plant grew 5 tomatoes. There were four plants. Draw a picture to show how many tomatoes Ashton grew. Solve.

_____ **tomatoes**

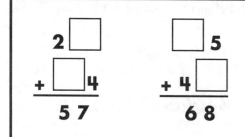

$$2\,\square$$
$$+\;\square\,4$$
$$\overline{5\,7}$$

$$\square\,5$$
$$+\;4\,\square$$
$$\overline{6\,8}$$

$$7\,8$$
$$+\;\square\,\square$$
$$\overline{9\,9}$$

$$6\,\square$$
$$+\;\square\,3$$
$$\overline{1\,0\,8}$$

$42 \div$ _____ $= 7$

$6 \times \square = 54$

$54 \div \square = 6$

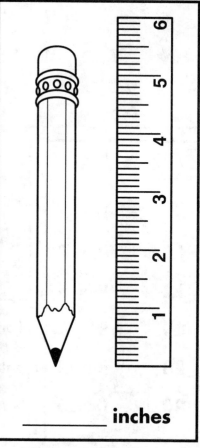

456
253
+ 178

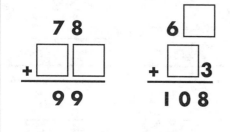

Break the circle into eighths. Label each part.

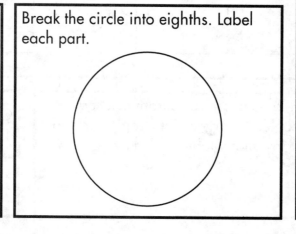

_____ **inches**

Jasmine collected seashells at the beach. She made 4 piles with 9 seashells in each pile. How many seashells did she collect in all?

Mrs. Witt bought 5 rolls of stickers. Each roll came with 50 stickers. How many stickers did she buy?

2,519
Rounded to the nearest hundred: _____

What fraction is shaded?

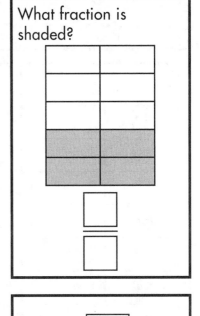

$32 \div 8 = \bigcirc$

$\bigcirc \div 4 = \bigcirc$

$\bigcirc \div \bigcirc = 8$

$14 \div \bigcirc = \bigcirc$

$35 \div \bigcirc = \bigcirc$

$20 \div \bigcirc = \bigcirc$

$24 \div 6 = \bigcirc$

_____ × _____ = _____

$54 \div \boxed{} = 9$

$\boxed{} \times 9 = 54$

$54 \div 9 = \boxed{}$

$9 \times \boxed{} = 54$

Draw a picture to show 24 ÷ 6. Write an equation to match.

2 × 4 × 3 =
_____ **× (4×3)**

232
457
+ 281

Name _____

A café sells sandwiches for $3, drinks for $2, and fruit for $1. Amir bought one sandwich, one drink, and two pieces of fruit. How much did he spend?

÷ 6	
36	
18	
12	
60	
48	
24	
30	
42	
54	

×	2	3	4	5	6
2					
3					
4					
5					
6					

$$592 + 148$$

Grant's brother turned 18 years old in 2015. What year was he born?

_____

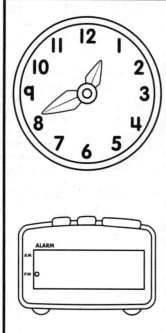

____ ◯ ____

Count the tiles to find the area.

area = _____ square units

_____, 210, 310, _____, _____

_____ rows of _____ = _____

Three friends shared 15 gumballs equally.

○ **15 ÷ 3**

○ **3 × 15**

○ **15 ÷ 5**

Connect the dots to form a square. Divide it into fourths.

· · · · ·
· · · · ·
· · · · ·
· · · · ·
· · · · ·

Solve. Color the products with an even number red. Color the products with an odd number blue.

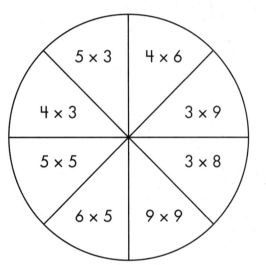

72 ÷ _____ = 9

Add the sides to find the perimeter.

22 m

10 m ▭ 10 m

22 m

perimeter = _____ m

Draw a line to match.

8)‾6‾4‾	5
7)‾4‾9‾	2
6)‾3‾6‾	8
5)‾2‾5‾	7
4)‾1‾6‾	3
3)‾9‾	2
2)‾4‾	6
1)‾2‾	4

What time will it be in 2 hours and 30 minutes?

What is the only quadrilateral with four right angles and four equal sides? Draw an example.

Which would you use to measure the mass of an apple?

gram   kilogram

248 = ◯ **2 hundreds + 48 tens**

◯ **2 hundreds + 48 ones**

◯ **2 hundreds + 40 tens + 8 ones**

Shayna left her house at 10:10 am. She went to the gym, post office, and grocery store. She was gone for 2 hours and 35 minutes. What time did she get home?

9 × 9 = ▢

▢ **÷ 9 = 9**

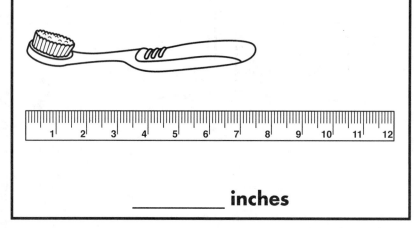

_____ **inches**

How many pink? _____

How many more red than orange?

_____

How many whites and red combined? _____

2,997 is about _____ thousands.

3 × 60 = ▢

60 × 3 = ▢

▢ **÷ 3 = 60**

▢ **÷ 60 = 3**

Leo had 18 friends over for a party. His mom made two dozen cupcakes. Does Leo have enough cupcakes for him and his friends to each have one? Does he have enough for his mom, dad, and 2 younger sisters to also have one? Show your work.

```
 H T O
 3 0 2
-1 5 4
```

Solve. Circle the three problems in a row that have the same answer.

15 ÷ 5	14 ÷ 2	20 ÷ 4
12 ÷ 4	9 ÷ 3	16 ÷ 4
6 ÷ 3	16 ÷ 4	6 ÷ 2

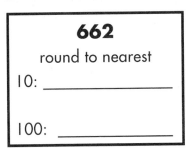

_____ ÷ _____ = _____

Rafi sold 450 tickets for the raffle. Ed sold 265 tickets. How many more tickets did Rafi sell than Ed?

433	
	102

× 7	
2	
6	
9	
7	
8	
5	
1	
4	
3	
0	
10	

What time is it? _____

What time will it be in a half hour?

_____

What time will it be in 1 $\frac{1}{2}$ hours?

_____

What time will it be in 2 $\frac{1}{2}$ hours?

_____

area = _____
square units

$7 \times$ _____ $= 42$

_____ $\times 7 = 42$

$42 \div$ _____ $= 7$

$42 \div 7 =$ _____

518 + 355 = _____

662
round to nearest

10: _____

100: _____

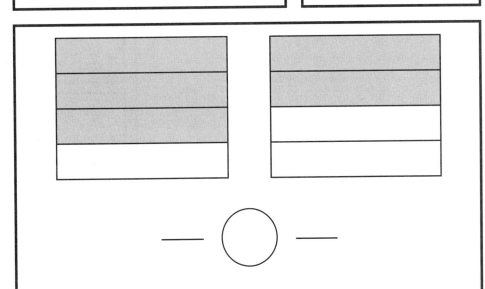

_____ ◯ _____

45 divided into 5 equal groups equals:

◯ 5

◯ 9

◯ 45

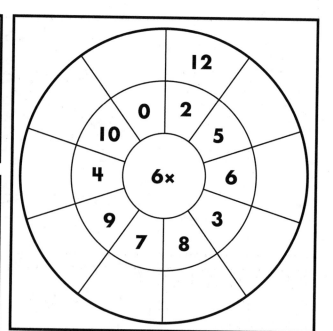

Draw a line to match.

6 × 3	28
4 × 5	18
8 × 3	30
7 × 4	42
8 × 6	36
6 × 7	20
9 × 4	48
6 × 5	24

Kevin downloaded 3 songs. His sister Carrie downloaded 4 more songs than Kevin did. How many songs did they download in all?

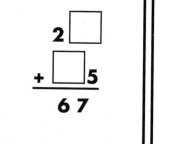

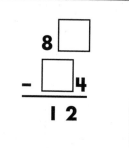

Kara has 2 dogs. She has 10 dog biscuits. She finds 2 more biscuits. If she shares the biscuits evenly, how many biscuits will each dog get?

Each dog will get ___ biscuits.

Draw an array to solve.

6 × 4 = _____

78 + 21 is about _____.

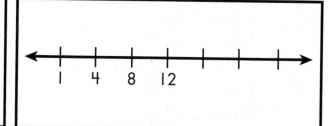

A fish tank holds

○ **less than 1 liter.**

○ **about 1 liter.**

○ **more than 1 liter.**

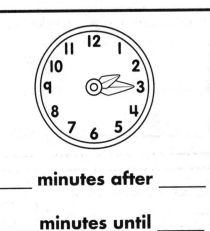

_____ **minutes after** _____

_____ **minutes until** _____

Solve. Color the flag.
6's = green
7's = yellow
8's = blue

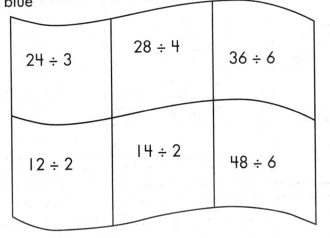

24 ÷ 3

28 ÷ 4

36 ÷ 6

12 ÷ 2

14 ÷ 2

48 ÷ 6

$\boxed{} \div 8 = 6$, so $6 \times 8 = \boxed{}$.

Add the sides to find the perimeter.

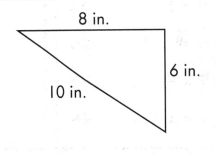

8 in.

6 in.

10 in.

perimeter = _____ in.

0 × 10	
1 × 10	
2 × 10	
3 × 10	
4 × 10	
5 × 10	
6 × 10	
7 × 10	
8 × 10	
9 × 10	
10 × 10	

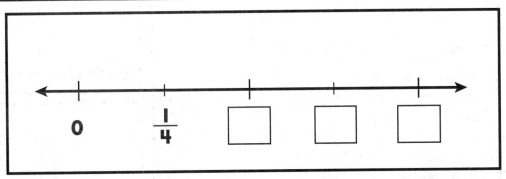

0 $\dfrac{1}{4}$ ☐   ☐   ☐

$3 \times 5 \times 2 = (3 \times \underline{}) \times 2$

I have five sides and five angles. Who am I? Draw me.

Complete the model to show 24 ÷ 4.

24			
		6	

_____ ÷ _____ = _____

Andy has 16 gumballs. He eats 2. He wants to share the rest equally with his brother. How many gumballs will each boy get?

2,167
Round to nearest

10: _____

100: _____

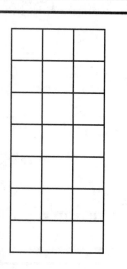

area = _____ square units

What time is it? _____

What time will it be in 30 minutes? _____

What time will it be in 50 minutes? _____

What time will it be in 1 $\frac{1}{2}$ hours? _____

56 ÷ 8 = _____

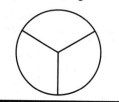

Color to show $\frac{3}{3}$.

÷ 3	
24	
15	
27	
18	
21	

Kim made an array using counters. Her array had four rows with 6 counters in each row. How many counters did she use in her array?

Write a number in the square to complete the fact triangle.

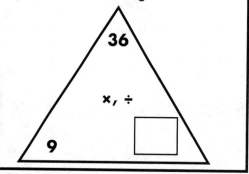

_____ × _____ = _____

There are 32 adults and 19 kids in the theater. About how many people in all are in the theater?

_____

5 × _____ = 40

The market sells baskets of apples for $3. Each basket holds 8 apples. Emma buys 16 total apples. How much did she spend?

15 ÷ 5 =	
12 ÷ 4 =	
8 ÷ 4 =	
24 ÷ 4 =	
25 ÷ 5 =	
16 ÷ 4 =	
20 ÷ 4 =	
30 ÷ 5 =	

Solve. Color the even products blue and the odd products red.

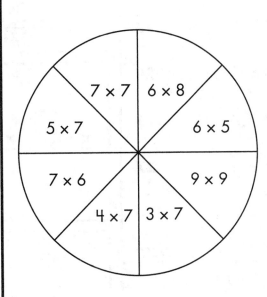

There are 20 students in Mr. Greene's class. Each student has 3 folders in their desks. How many folders are there in all?

45 ÷ 9 = _____

600
– 459

Draw a model to match 30 ÷ 6.

623, _____, _____, 683, _____

Solve. Circle the three problems in a row that have the same answer.

12 ÷ 2	3 × 8	24 ÷ 3
24 ÷ 6	12 ÷ 4	3 × 4
4 × 6	8 × 3	6 × 4

28 ÷ 7	3
24 ÷ 6	4
21 ÷ 3	6
27 ÷ 9	7
24 ÷ 4	9
27 ÷ 3	3
21 ÷ 7	6

7 × 3	24
6 × 4	21
8 × 3	27
9 × 3	24
3 × 7	21
4 × 6	27
3 × 9	24

$$
\begin{array}{r} 3 \\ \times\,10 \\ \hline \end{array}
\qquad
\begin{array}{r} 3 \\ \times\,20 \\ \hline \end{array}
$$

$$
\begin{array}{r} 400 \\ -\,257 \\ \hline \end{array}
$$

Connect the dots to form a rectangle. Divide it into thirds.

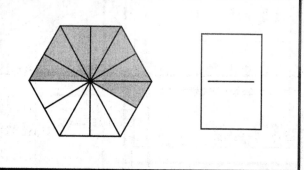

248 + 589 = _____

Four friends spent $36 on tickets for the carnival. They each bought their own tickets plus $3 game passes. How much did each friend spend?

Each square = 1 cm

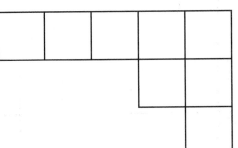

area = _____ square cm

Split the hexagon into sixths.
Label each piece.

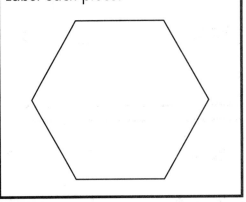

I am a quadrilateral with only one pair of parallel sides.

Who am I? _____

Draw me.

54 ÷ _____ = 6

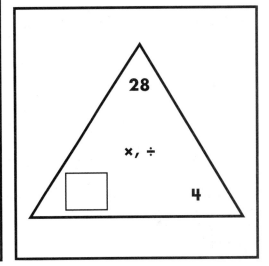

28

×, ÷

4

36 ÷ 4 = _____

48 ÷ 6 = _____

42 ÷ 7 = _____

54 ÷ 9 = _____

35 ÷ 5 = _____

Use the number line to solve.
Start time: 11:15 am   End time: 1:25 pm   Elapsed time: _____

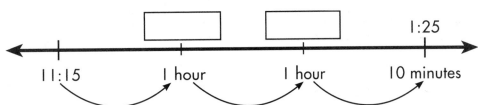

Write the whole number as a fraction.

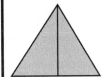

2 = ——

652
+ 342

542 – 189 = ○ 500 – 100

○ 500 – 200

○ 600 – 200

Shelby and her friends take 2 small coolers to the beach. Each cooler holds 8 water bottles. How many water bottles did they bring in all?

777
Round to nearest

10: _____

100: _____

Books Read

June	📖 📖 📖 📖
July	📖 📖 📖
August	📖 📖 📖

Key: 📖 = 2 students

In which month were the most books read?

_____

How many books were read in August?

_____

How many more books were read in June than in July?

_____

6	× 3	
5	× 3	
4	× 3	
3	× 3	
2	× 3	

7 × _____ = 49

| 345 | |
| 144 | |

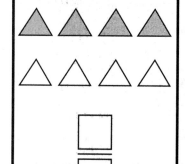

18 ÷ 3 = _____

The divisor is _____.

The dividend is _____.

The quotient is _____.

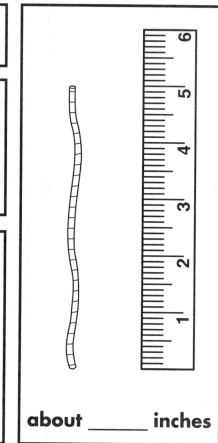

about _____ inches

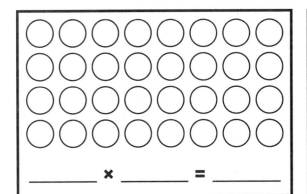

_____ × _____ = _____

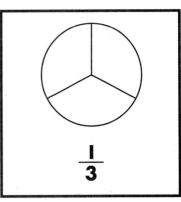

$\dfrac{1}{3}$

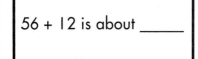

56 + 12 is about _____

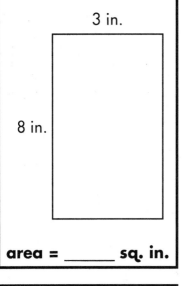

3 in.

8 in.

area = _____ sq. in.

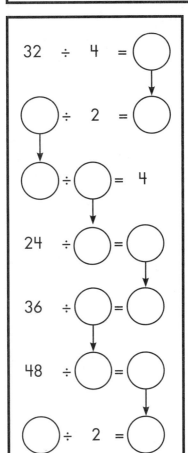

32 ÷ 4 = ◯

◯ ÷ 2 = ◯

◯ ÷ ◯ = 4

24 ÷ ◯ = ◯

36 ÷ ◯ = ◯

48 ÷ ◯ = ◯

◯ ÷ 2 = ◯

Aaron leaves for basketball practice at 4:00 pm. It takes him 10 minutes to ride his bike to practice, 60 minutes to practice, and 10 minutes to ride his bike home. What time did he get home? Show your work.

423
235
+ 89

602 − 425 = _____

6 × 4 = _____

6 × 40 = _____

4 × 6 = _____

4 × 60 = _____

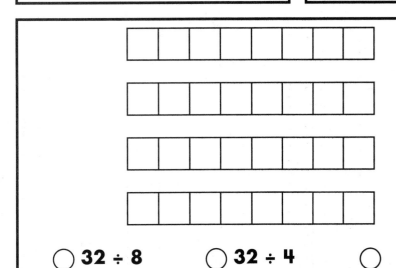

◯ **32 ÷ 8**   ◯ **32 ÷ 4**   ◯ **8 ÷ 4**

Six ice pops come in a box. There are 18 girls on the track team. How many boxes do they need to buy so every girl can have an ice pop?

_____ boxes

7 × 3	
6 × 5	
7 × 4	
5 × 3	
3 × 6	
6 × 4	
7 × 8	
8 × 4	
9 × 3	
6 × 6	

÷ 3	
9	3
24	
12	
15	
30	
6	
18	
21	
27	
3	

Baseball practice starts at 1:30 pm. The clock shows what time practice ended. How long was practice? _____ hour and _____ minutes

A bucket of water holds about:

5 liters

5 grams

A pencil weighs:

1 gram

1 pound

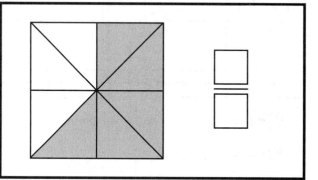

452 + 32 + 148 = _____

30 ÷ 5 = _____

The dividend is _____.

The divisor is _____.

The quotient is _____.

Shared among 4 friends, each friend gets _____ star cookies.

_____ **minutes after 6**

_____ **minutes until 7**

Shayla had $20. She bought 2 books for $6 each. How much money did she have left?

_____

×	6	7	8	9	10
2					
3					
4					
5					
6					

633 – 485 = _____

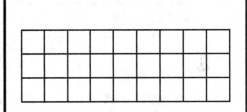

1 square = 1 cm

area = _____ square cm

$9\overline{)81}$ = _____

$9\overline{)72}$ = _____

$9\overline{)63}$ = _____

$9\overline{)54}$ = _____

$9\overline{)45}$ = _____

$9\overline{)36}$ = _____

$9\overline{)27}$ = _____

$9\overline{)18}$ = _____

$9\overline{)9}$ = _____

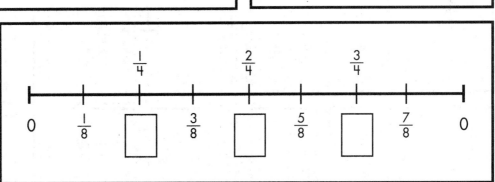

There are 52 boys and 56 girls in the third grade. About how many students is that in all?

_____ + _____ = _____

$(3×2) × 4 = 3 × (2 + 4)$

true   false

638 + 383 = ○ 600 + 300

○ 600 + 400

○ 700 + 400

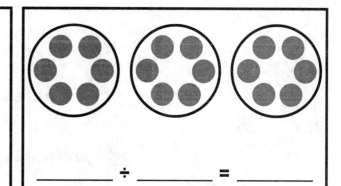

_____ ÷ _____ = _____

A photo album has 10 pages with 4 photos on each page. How many photos does the photo album hold in all?

Write a story to solve 24 ÷ 6.

_____

_____

_____

_____

Peyton leaves her house at 10:00 am. She rides her bike for 15 minutes to her friend's house. They watch a movie for an hour and 30 minutes and eat lunch for 30 minutes. Then, Peyton rides back home for 15 minutes. What time does she get home?

56 ÷ 7 = _____

300
− 124

6 × 4	
4 × 4	
7 × 4	
9 × 4	
10 × 4	
3 × 4	
8 × 4	
2 × 4	
0 × 4	
5 × 4	

Color to show $\frac{2}{3}$.

Draw a three-sided polygon.

☐ ☐ ☐ ☐
☐ ☐ ☐ ☐
☐ ☐ ☐ ☐

_____ × _____ = _____

8 × 10 = _____

8 × 20 = _____

8 × 30 = _____

8 × 40 = _____

578 is about

_____ hundreds.

16 ÷ 2 = _____

28 ÷ 4 = _____

30 ÷ 5 = _____

15 ÷ 3 = _____

24 ÷ 6 = _____

18 ÷ 6 = _____

12 ÷ 6 = _____

9 ÷ 9 = _____

about _____ inches

2 × 6	= _____
_____ =	3 × 6
4 × 3	= _____
_____ =	4 × 6
3 × 5	= _____
_____ =	4 × 4

906
− 478

4 × _____ = 28

7 × 6 = ☐

☐ × 7 = 42

42 ÷ ☐ = 7

42 ÷ 7 = ☐

The clock shows what time Ethan finished swim practice. Practice started at 3:15 pm. How long was swim practice?

_____ hour _____ minutes

Kyle and Nate are playing basketball. Kyle has scored twice as many points as Nate. Nate has scored 9 points. How much has Kyle scored?

64 ÷ 8	7
42 ÷ 6	4
56 ÷ 7	9
63 ÷ 9	8
54 ÷ 6	8
28 ÷ 7	7

How many 9s are in 45? Draw a picture to solve.

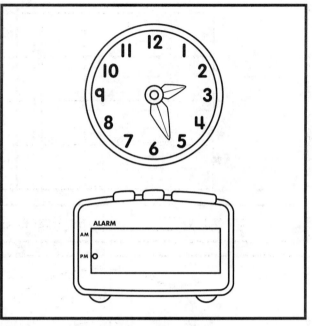

206 − 128	496 + 257

4 × 6 = _____

Draw an array to match.

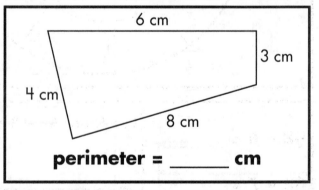

perimeter = _____ cm

47 + 32 is about _____.

Mia buys two shirts for $6 each. She buys a pair of shorts for $8 and a hat for $4. How much does she spend?

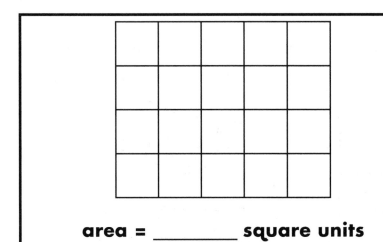

area = _____ square units

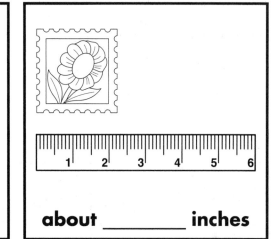

about _____ inches

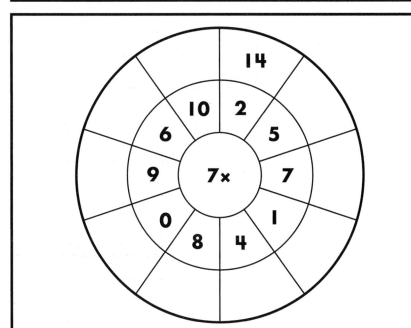

_____, 510, 530, _____, _____

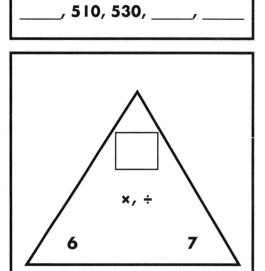

48 ÷ 6 = _____

63 ÷ 7 = _____

35 ÷ 5 = _____

24 ÷ 6 = _____

14 ÷ 2 = _____

10 ÷ 10 = _____

Locate and label the fractions on the number line: 0, $\frac{1}{4}$, $\frac{2}{4}$, $\frac{3}{4}$, 1.

⟵——————————————————⟶

Circle the set of parallel lines.

$\frac{1}{2}$ ◯ $\frac{5}{10}$

731 + 269 is about ◯ **700 + 270.**

◯ **730 + 260.**

◯ **730 + 270.**

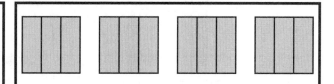

$$\frac{12}{3} = \boxed{}$$

---

5 × 3 × 4 = 5 × (3 × 4)

true   **false**

What time does the clock show? _____

What time will it be in 20 minutes? _____

What time was it 20 minutes ago? _____

One swimming pool can hold 63 L of water and another can hold 59 L of water. What is the difference between the two pools?

_____ **L**

56 ÷ _____ = 8

609

round to nearest

10: _____

100: _____

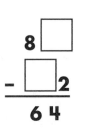

Kenzi had 3 packs of bubblegum. Each pack had 10 pieces in it. She gave 8 pieces to her sister. How many pieces of gum did she have left? _____

1 ÷ 1 = ☐

2 ÷ 1 = ☐

2 ÷ 2 = ☐

3 ÷ 1 = ☐

3 ÷ 3 = ☐

4 ÷ 1 = ☐

4 ÷ 4 = ☐

5 ÷ 1 = ☐

5 ÷ 5 = ☐

Draw a picture to solve **18 ÷ 3**.

☐ **× 6 = 54**

54 ÷ ☐ **= 6**

☐ **= _____**

879 is about _____ hundreds.

0 × 0	
1 × 1	
2 × 2	
3 × 3	
4 × 4	
5 × 5	
6 × 6	
7 × 7	
8 × 8	
9 × 9	
10 × 10	

Xander's mom buys 3 bananas, 4 oranges, and 4 apples at the market. When they get home, Xander eats one banana and his brother eats an apple. How many pieces of fruit are left? _____

_____ × _____ = _____

How many legs are on

1 spider? _____

2 spiders? _____

5 spiders? _____

10 spiders? _____

369 + 885 = _____

one paper clip
weighs about

1 gram

1 kilogram

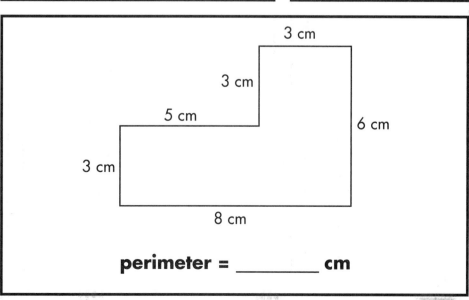

perimeter = _____ cm

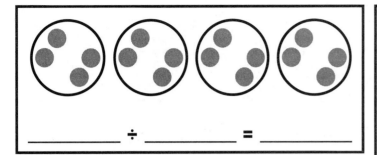

_____ ÷ _____ = _____

There are 98 third graders going on the field trip. Of the group, 62 students are bringing a packed lunch, and the rest are buying lunch from the cafeteria. How many students are buying lunch from the cafeteria?

÷ 4	
4	
24	
16	
8	
32	
12	
36	
40	
20	

6 × 2 = _____

2 × 5 = _____

5 × 6 = _____

6 × 3 = _____

3 × 7 = _____

7 × 6 = _____

3 × 10 = _____

3 × 20 = _____

3 × 30 = _____

$$\begin{array}{r} 600 \\ -\ 284 \\ \hline \end{array}$$

633	
125	

762, _____, 722, 702, _____

Draw an array to match 3 × 8 = _____.

Use addition to fill in the boxes.

```
        119
      [  ] 64
     [ ] 32 [ ]
   [ ] 15 [ ] [ ]
  [ ] 7  8 [ ] [ ]
```

	5	

|← 15 →|

A garbage truck can hold about

○ **1 liter.**

○ **10 liters.**

○ **10,000 liters.**

Jazmyn packed four lunch bags for her picnic with her cousins. Each bag had 6 snacks inside. She gave one bag full of snacks to her brother. How many snacks did she have left for the picnic? Draw a picture to solve.

56 ÷ 7 = _____

×	2	4	6
3			
5			
7			

2 × 3 =	
	= 4 × 3
5 × 3 =	
	= 6 × 3

Divide into fourths. Label each fourth. Plot Point A at $\frac{3}{4}$.

←————|————————————————————|————→
    0   1

5 in.

3 in.

area = _____ sq. inches

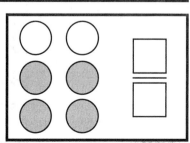

648 − 364 is about ◯ **600 − 350.**

◯ **650 − 400.**

◯ **650 − 360.**

Paolo went to the beach at 10:15 am. The clock shows the time when he got home. How long was he at the beach?

_____ hours _____ minutes

If 81 ÷ 9 = 9,

then 9 × 9 = ⬚ .

blue	
yellow	
red	

Key: ✏ = 2 crayons

Use the key to complete the picture graph to match the data.

blue = 6 crayons

yellow = 4 crayons

red = 8 crayons

Solve. Color even products green. Color odd products yellow.

3 × 5	5 × 5
9 × 3	7 × 7
7 × 6	5 × 8
4 × 8	6 × 6
3 × 7	9 × 7
4 × 5	6 × 8

783 is about _____ hundreds.

Your thumb is about

_____ inches long.

$4\overline{)16}$	7
$9\overline{)81}$	3
$3\overline{)27}$	7
$7\overline{)21}$	6
$8\overline{)48}$	9
$7\overline{)56}$	8
$9\overline{)63}$	5
$7\overline{)49}$	7
$4\overline{)20}$	4

$$\begin{array}{r} 368 \\ 361 \\ + \ 226 \\ \hline \end{array}$$

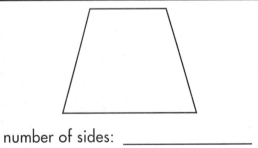

number of sides: _____

number of corners: _____

name of shape: _____

9⟌63

The dividend is _____.

The divisor is _____.

The quotient is _____.

Five baskets of 6 eggs equals _____ eggs in all.

$5 \times 7 = 7 + 5$

true   false

How many 5s are in

30? _____

35? _____

40? _____

45? _____

Miquel left his house at 3:20 pm. He rode his bike 20 minutes, played at his friend's house for 40 minutes, and then rode back home for 20 minutes. What time did he get home? Draw your answer on the clock.

```
  236
  451
+ 278
```

$64 \div 8 =$ _____

☐ $\times\ 8 = 24$

$24 \div$ ☐ $= 8$

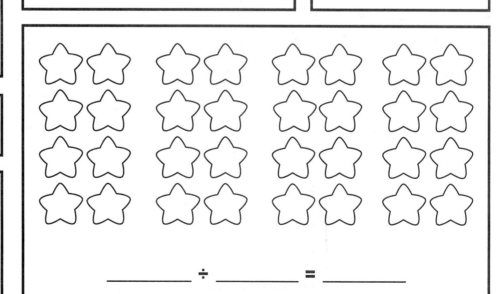

_____ ÷ _____ = _____

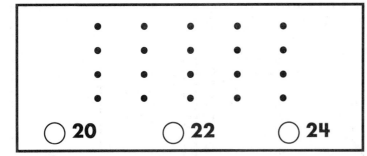

○ **20**   ○ **22**   ○ **24**

Kaylee is learning how to sew. She is making a quilt that has 4 rows. Each row has 6 squares of fabric. How many squares of fabric does Kaylee need to make her quilt?

3 × 4 =	
2 × 9 =	
1 × 6 =	
7 × 4 =	
9 × 5 =	
7 × 8 =	

	÷ 6
12	
36	
48	
6	
30	
42	
54	

$$300 - 189$$

$$656 + 325$$

Jack made 3 outs in his baseball game on Wednesday. On Thursday, he made twice as many outs. In his Saturday game, he made one less than Thursday. How many outs did he make in these three games?

Circle the multiplication facts. Hint: There is one diagonal fact!

6	2	12	6
5	3	3	1
2	6	12	6
10	2	4	8

1, 2, 4, _____, _____

728
Round to nearest

10: _____

100: _____

Beth is 56 inches tall. Her brother Jim is 4 inches taller than her. Her sister Sarah is 2 inches shorter than Jim. How tall are Jim and Sarah?

A large bottle of soda is

less than one liter.

more than one liter.

Draw a picture to solve 36 ÷ 6 = _____ .

245 – 178 = _____

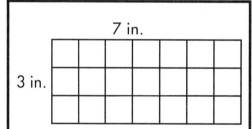

7 in.

3 in.

area = _____ sq. in.

2 × 4	
4 × 4	
6 × 4	
8 × 4	
10 × 4	

Marcus started his homework at 4:30 pm. He worked for 45 minutes, then ate a 30-minute dinner. What time did he finish his dinner? Use the number line to solve.

6			

⊢————— 24 —————⊣

60 × 4 = _____
2 × 30 = _____
6 × 40 = _____
3 × 20 = _____

Draw a quadrilateral that is **not** a rectangle.

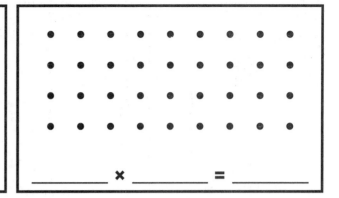

_____ × _____ = _____

How many 4s are in

16? _____

24? _____

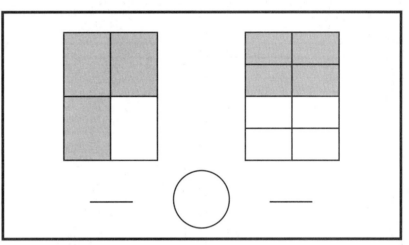

_____   ◯   _____

Paige does her homework right before dinner. She reads for 30 minutes. Then, she does her math homework for 20 minutes. Dinner starts at 5:45 pm. What time did she start her homework?

---

312 is about _____ hundreds.

```
H T O
4 5 8
- 3 6 9
```

12	÷ 3	
24	÷ 3	
15	÷ 3	
21	÷ 3	
30	÷ 3	
27	÷ 3	
6	÷ 3	
9	÷ 3	

```
  256
   67
+ 457
```

Mrs. Jameson paid $302 for a plane ticket to visit her sister. Mr. Kelly went on a business trip and paid $376 for his plane ticket. Who paid more? How much more?

Zoe goes to the arcade with $3 in her pocket. If she can play four games for $1, how many games can she play for $3?

9 × 10 = _____

9 × 20 = _____

9 × 30 = _____

9 × 40 = _____

235 + 630 = _____

ounces

pounds

Color the path of the even products.

START	
2 × 3	5 × 5
4 × 4	6 × 2
3 × 7	2 × 8
9 × 3	8 × 3
6 × 4	6 × 3
2 × 7	3 × 5
4 × 5	6 × 5
7 × 7	2 × 10
FINISH	

_____ minutes past _____

_____ minutes to _____

Color $\frac{6}{9}$.

Javon had 4 bags of candy. Each bag had 9 pieces of candy in it. He ate 3 pieces of candy and gave 3 pieces to his sister. How many pieces of candy were left? Show your work.

28 ÷ _____ = 7

How many wheels on

1 car? _____

2 cars? _____

3 cars? _____

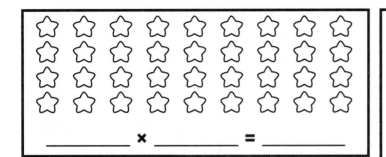

_____ × _____ = _____

12 ÷ 3	
4 × 3	
12 ÷ 4	
6 ÷ 3	
6 × 2	
12 ÷ 6	

6 × 2	
6 ÷ 2	
3 × 4	
2 × 6	
12 ÷ 2	
6 ÷ 1	

Add to find the perimeter.

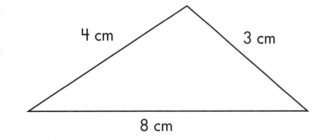

4 cm   3 cm

8 cm

perimeter = _____ cm

What time does the clock show?

_____

What time was it 15 minutes ago?

_____

What time will it be in 15 minutes?

_____

504
- 458

235
+ 398

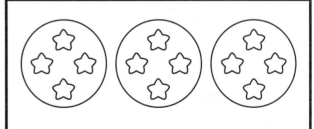

12 ÷ _____ = _____

335, _____, 355, _____, _____

Jillian had 32 stickers. She shared them evenly among herself and her 3 friends. How many stickers did each friend get?

Rowan gets home from school at 3:05 pm. He plays in his backyard for 30 minutes, then comes inside and reads for 20 minutes. Afterward, he plays on the computer for 25 minutes. What time is it now?

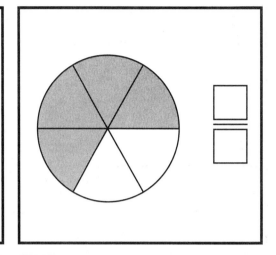

×	7	8	9	10
2				
3				
4				
5				

689 is about _____ hundreds.

Draw lines from the circled number to the quotients that match.

$12 \div 6$ $6 \div 2$ $4 \div 2$

$14 \div 2$ (2) $20 \div 4$

$14 \div 7$ $10 \div 5$

$16 \div 8$ $12 \div 6$ $12 \div 4$

$8\overline{)64}$ = _____

$4\overline{)36}$ = _____

$7\overline{)28}$ = _____

$8\overline{)32}$ = _____

$5\overline{)25}$ = _____

$7\overline{)21}$ = _____

Plot the fractions on the number line.

$A = \frac{1}{4}$, $B = \frac{1}{2}$, $C = \frac{3}{4}$, $D = 1$

⟵———————————————————⟶

Multiply to find the area.

8 cm

3 cm [ ]

area = _____ sq. cm

H	T	O
4	7	2
– 2	8	6

Amy shared 36 crayons equally between 6 friends. How many did each friend get?

○ **4 each**

○ **5 each**

○ **6 each**

A jar of jellybeans holds more than 20 but less than 30 jellybeans. You can divide the jellybeans equally into groups of 4. There are more than 25 jellybeans in the jar. How many jellybeans are in the jar?

(2 + 4) + 6 = 2 + (_____ + 6)

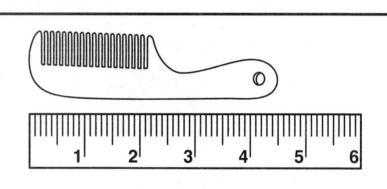

_____ **inches**

Break the rectangle into six equal parts. Label each part.

_____ = **4 × 8**

$\dfrac{2}{4} = \dfrac{\boxed{}}{2}$

15 ÷ 3 =	
	= 12 ÷ 4
24 ÷ 4 =	
	= 16 ÷ 8
20 ÷ 4 =	
	= 16 ÷ 4
28 ÷ 7 =	

223
611
+ 138

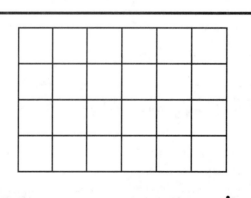

area = _____ square units

755 + 115 is about

○ **700 + 100.**

○ **750 + 110.**

○ **760 + 120.**

Forty-two marbles shared equally with six children is _____ marbles for each child.

7 × _____ = 35

quarter past 8

quarter till 9

Color the path of the odd quotients.

START	
4 ÷ 2	15 ÷ 5
10 ÷ 5	15 ÷ 3
25 ÷ 5	24 ÷ 8
27 ÷ 3	8 ÷ 2
9 ÷ 3	6 ÷ 3
30 ÷ 6	81 ÷ 9
42 ÷ 7	36 ÷ 4
18 ÷ 3	12 ÷ 4
FINISH	

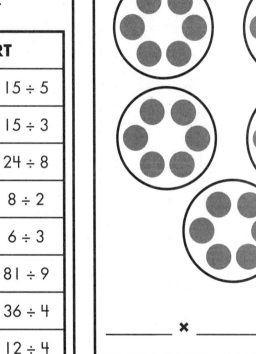

_____ **×** _____ **=** _____

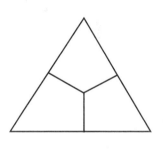

Color to show $\frac{3}{3}$.

9 × _____ = 63

Write a story to solve 54 ÷ 9 = _____.

_____

_____

_____

_____

_____

_____ **÷** _____ **=** _____

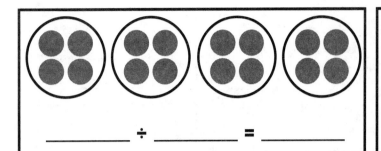

_____ ÷ _____ = _____

4 × 2	14
6 × 4	36
7 × 2	8
8 × 5	24
3 × 4	42
3 × 9	40
6 × 7	12
6 × 6	27

14 ÷ 7	6
24 ÷ 6	8
8 ÷ 2	2
40 ÷ 5	4
12 ÷ 4	3
27 ÷ 9	4
42 ÷ 7	3
36 ÷ 6	6

Marco's soccer practice started at 4:10 pm. Practice was an hour and half long. What time did practice end? Draw your answer on the clock.

```
  234
   24
+ 234
```

```
  610
- 458
```

Maria bought two books at $8 each and a pack of pens for $3. She paid with a $20 bill. How much change did she get back?

Circle the division facts.

30	5	6	12
10	12	2	2
5	6	3	6
2	2	1	4

621 + 310 is about _____ hundreds.

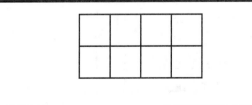

area = _____ square units

_____ ÷ _____ = _____

Kevin went to the movies. The movie started at 7:10 pm and ended at 9:26 pm. How long was the movie?

_____ hr. _____ min.

Favorite Ice Cream

What is the title of this bar graph? _____

Which flavor had the most votes? _____

How many more people voted for vanilla than strawberry? _____

301 – 103 = _____

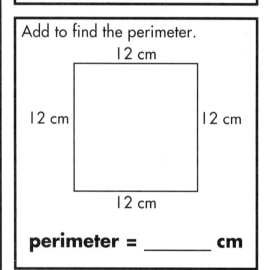

Add to find the perimeter.

12 cm

12 cm   12 cm

12 cm

perimeter = _____ cm

Vance has 42 mL of liquid in his science beaker. Becca has 38 mL. Whose beaker has more liquid? How much more?

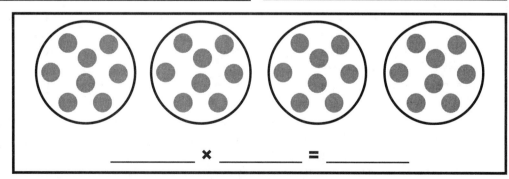

_____ × _____ = _____

>, <, or =

This is a right angle.

true   false

637 − 475 is about ◯ **140.**

◯ **160.**

◯ **200.**

Draw a picture to solve 32 ÷ 4 = _____.

If 9 × 8 = 72,

then 72 ÷ ▢ = 8.

The pet store has 5 fish tanks. There are 10 fish in each tank. On Saturday, 8 fish were sold. On Sunday, 14 fish were sold. How many fish were left?

Add to find the perimeter.

7 in.

4 in.

5 in.

6 in.

perimeter = _____ in.

---

56 ÷ 8 = _____

---

10 × 4 = _____

20 × 4 = _____

30 × 4 = _____

---

15 ÷ 3 =	
	= 6 × 4
12 ÷ 2 =	
	= 4 × 5
24 ÷ 3 =	
	= 8 × 2
18 ÷ 3 =	
	= 4 × 3

113
564
+ 26

Isaiah rode his bike 15 minutes to the basketball courts, played basketball for 1 hour 15 minutes, and then rode his bike 15 minutes home. He left his house at 9:20 am. What time did he get home?

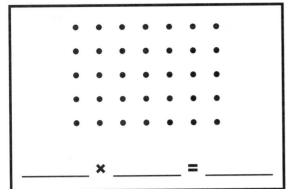

_____ × _____ = _____

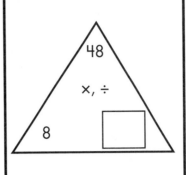

$18 \div \underline{\hspace{2cm}} = 9$

Martin saw a stop sign at the corner of his street. He said it was a pentagon. Do you agree with him? Why or why not?

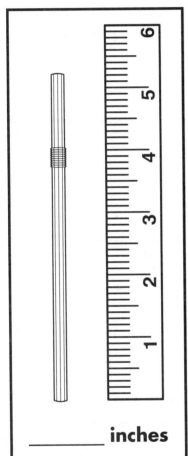

_____ inches

Kirsten participated in a read-a-thon. She read 158 pages in Week 1, 182 pages in Week 2, 177 pages in Week 3, and 189 pages in Week 4. Her goal was to read 700 pages in four weeks. Did she reach her goal?

$6 \times 7 = \underline{\hspace{2cm}}$

$\underline{\hspace{2cm}} \times 6 = 42$

$\underline{\hspace{2cm}} \div 7 = 6$

$42 \div \underline{\hspace{2cm}} = 7$

$640 - 458 = \underline{\hspace{1.5cm}}$

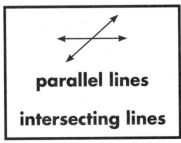

parallel lines

intersecting lines

Leigh went to bed at 9:15 pm. The clock shows what time she woke up in the morning. How long did she sleep?

_____ **hours and** _____ **minutes.**

$$900$$
$$- \ 189$$

○ **811**

○ **721**

○ **711**

Austin had 2 bowls of blueberries. There were 9 blueberries in each bowl. He ate 7 blueberries. How many were left? Draw a picture to show your work.

0 × 5	
1 × 6	
2 × 6	
5 × 1	
6 × 0	
2 × 5	
1 × 0	

2 × 3	
3 × 6	
2 × 8	
3 × 8	
6 × 2	
6 × 3	
8 × 3	

$$658$$
$$+ \ 231$$

$40 × 4 =$ _____

$60 × 3 =$ _____

$80 × 2 =$ _____

Multiply to find the area.

6 in.

3 in.

area = _____ in.

Draw an array to solve $5 × 7 =$ _____.

114, _____, 134, _____, _____

Jordan's game started at 6:05 pm. The game finished at 7:10 pm, and it took 20 minutes to get home. What time did Jordan get home?

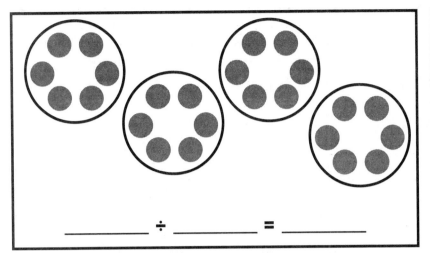

_____ ÷ _____ = _____

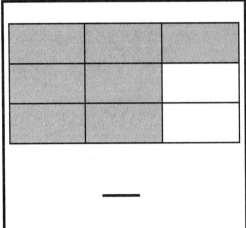

___

What time is it? _____

What time will it be in 1 hour and 10 minutes?

_____

What time was it 1 hour and 10 minutes ago?

_____

16 ÷ 2 = _____

There were four trees in Evan's backyard. He counted 4 birds in each tree. Then, 4 birds flew away. How many birds were left?

12 ÷ 2	2
12 ÷ 4	2
12 ÷ 3	3
14 ÷ 2	4
14 ÷ 7	4
16 ÷ 4	6
16 ÷ 8	7

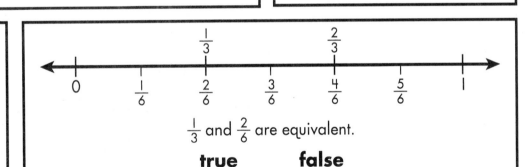

$\frac{1}{3}$ and $\frac{2}{6}$ are equivalent.

true   **false**

grams

kilograms

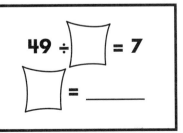

$49 ÷ \square = 7$

$\square = $ _____

A coffee mug holds

○ **about one liter.**

○ **less than one liter.**

○ **more than one liter.**

A ladybug has six legs. How many legs are on

2 ladybugs? _____

3 ladybugs? _____

4 ladybugs? _____

6, 12, 18, _____, _____

The concession stand at the little league field sells cheeseburgers for $3, hot dogs for $2, and drinks for $1. Cameron's family bought 2 cheeseburgers, 3 hot dogs, and 5 drinks. How much did they spend?

_____ minutes past _____

_____ minutes to _____

$64 \div$ _____ $= 8$

$7 \times 4 =$ _____ , so

$28 \div 4 =$ _____ .

$\div 4$	
24	
12	
4	
16	
32	
28	
36	

$$\begin{array}{r} 478 \\ -\ 289 \\ \hline \end{array}$$

Circle to show $12 \div 3 = 4$.

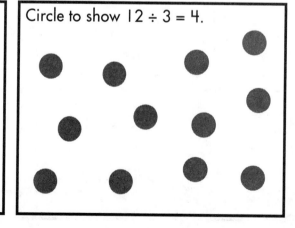

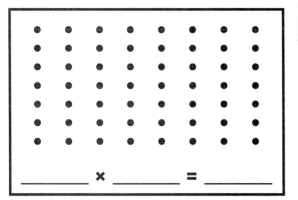

_____ **×** _____ = _____

amount of water
in a bathtub

mL

L

523 is about _____
hundreds.

A photo album holds
6 pictures per page
and has 10 pages in
the book. How many
pictures does each
album hold?

Follow the path of the
products with a **2** in
the ones place.

START	
6 × 2	7 × 4
1 × 2	5 × 3
4 × 8	6 × 7
4 × 2	9 × 8
8 × 2	2 × 6
6 × 4	4 × 3
FINISH	

Rob went to the movies. He left his
house at 3:00 pm, drove 15 minutes
to the movie theater, and watched a
movie that was $1\frac{1}{2}$ hours long. Then
he drove 15 minutes home. What
time did he get home? Show your
answer on the clock.

Thirty-six stamps

divided into 6 equal

groups equals

_____ stamps in

each group.

4 × _____ = 28

Show $\frac{4}{8}$.

Six groups of seven equals _____. Draw a picture to solve.

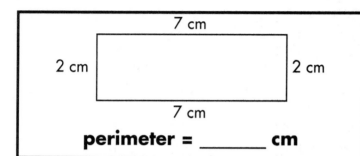

7 cm

2 cm   2 cm

7 cm

perimeter = _____ cm

Quinn has 2 pencil cases. Each pencil case has 8 pencils in it. How many pencils does he have in all?

8 × 6 = _____

7 × 6 = _____

6 × 6 = _____

5 × 6 = _____

4 × 6 = _____

3 × 6 = _____

2 × 6 = _____

1 × 6 = _____

18 ÷ 2 = _____

16 ÷ 2 = _____

14 ÷ 2 = _____

12 ÷ 2 = _____

10 ÷ 2 = _____

8 ÷ 2 = _____

6 ÷ 2 = _____

4 ÷ 2 = _____

2 ÷ 2 = _____

902
− 487
————

Fourteen stickers shared equally with 2 people equals _____ stickers per person.

Draw lines from the circled number to the problems that match.

12 ÷ 1   3 × 6   4 ÷ 3

6 × 2   2 × 6

12 ÷ 3   12 ÷ 2

3 × 4   12 × 1   12 ÷ 4

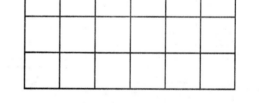

area = _____ square units

_____ × 2 × 3 = (1 × 2) × 3

18		
6		

_____ ÷ _____ = _____

Claire went to a party that lasted 3 hours and 20 minutes. The party started at 6:15 pm. What time did the party end?

○ **9:25**

○ **9:35**

○ **9:40**

Darius' mom bought 12 cookies for dessert. There are 4 people in her family. How many cookies will each person get?

Elana left her house at 11:40 am to meet a friend for lunch and go shopping. She got home 3 hours and 25 minutes later. What time did she get home? Show your answer on the clock.

---

425 + 475 = _____

Jack had 43 marbles. Paul had 58 marbles. About how many marbles did they have in all? Show your work.

$25 \div 5 =$ _____

$15 \div 5 =$ _____

$30 \div 5 =$ _____

$45 \div 5 =$ _____

$35 \div 5 =$ _____

$40 \div 5 =$ _____

$20 \div 5 =$ _____

Label the points: $\frac{1}{8}$, $\frac{2}{8}$, $\frac{3}{8}$, $\frac{4}{8}$, $\frac{5}{8}$, $\frac{6}{8}$, and $\frac{7}{8}$.

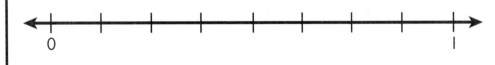

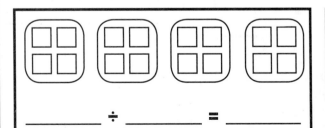

_____ ÷ _____ = _____

---

the mass of a bicycle

grams

kilograms

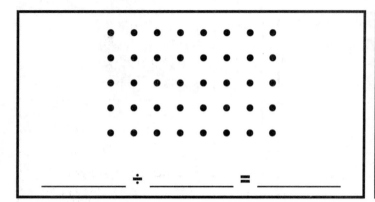

_____ ÷ _____ = _____

Four friends share 16 strawberries equally. How many strawberries does each friend get? Write a number sentence and solve.

3 baskets with
9 toys in each basket

_____ × _____ = _____

A recycling company collected 283 pounds of recyclable materials in week one, 211 pounds in week two, 249 pounds in week three, and 236 pounds in week four. How many pounds of recyclable materials did they collect that month?

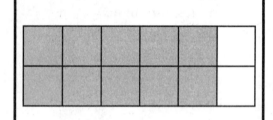

$54 ÷ 6 =$ _____

$3 × 2 = 3 + 2$

true   **false**

Makayla planted 6 flower pots in her windows. Each flower pot had 7 flowers. How many flowers did she plant in all? Draw a picture to solve the problem.

$5 × 50 =$ _____

$4 × 50 =$ _____

$3 × 50 =$ _____

$2 × 50 =$ _____

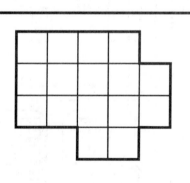

area = _____ **square units**

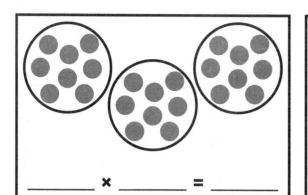

_____ × _____ = _____

25 ÷ 5

The divisor is _____.

The dividend is _____.

The quotient is _____.

500 – 48 = _____

Some friends shared 24 jellybeans. Each friend got 6 jellybeans. How many friends were there?

3 × 4 =	
	= 5 × 3
6 × 2 =	
	= 3 × 6
5 × 6 =	
	= 4 × 6
4 × 4 =	
	= 4 × 5

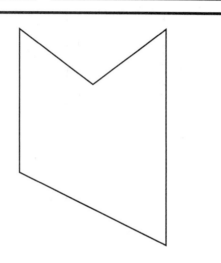

How many sides? _____

How many angles? _____

Name the shape. _____

20 counters

4 equal groups

_____ counters

in each group

The classroom had 4 rows of 6 desks. How many desks are there in all? Draw an array to match.

741 + 252 = _____

If 9 × 6 = 54, then

54 ÷ _____ = _____.

43 + 158 is about ◯ **180.**

◯ **200.**

◯ **220.**

```
  28
-  7
-----
  21
-  7
-----
  14
-  7
-----
   7
-  7
-----
   0
```

28 ÷ 7 = _____

```
  25
-  5
-----
  20
-  5
-----
  15
-  5
-----
  10
-  5
-----
   5
-  5
-----
   0
```

25 ÷ 5 = _____

Byron makes some sandwiches. Each sandwich uses 2 pieces of bread, 3 pieces of sliced turkey, and 1 slice of cheese. He makes 4 sandwiches. How many pieces of bread, turkey, and cheese does he use?

bread = _____

turkey = _____

cheese = _____

Your drawer holds 12 matching socks. How many pairs of socks can you make?

There are 8 pairs of socks. How many socks in all?

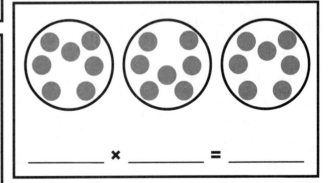

_____ **×** _____ = _____

Books Read

Who read the most books over the summer?

_____

How many more books did Myra read than Jon?

_____

The summer reading goal was to read at least 4 books. Who reached the goal? _____

632, _____, _____, 602, _____

Mr. McCormack buys 32 muffins for his staff meeting. The muffins come in packs of 4. How many packs does he buy?

Write a division sentence to match.

_____ ÷ _____ = _____

Some students shared a pack of 30 pencils. Each student got 5 pencils. How many students were there?

Ana went to the movies. The movie started at 2:50 pm. The clock shows what time it ended. How long was the movie?

---

24 ÷ _____ = 7

There are 36 counters and 4 equal groups. How many counters are in each group? Draw a picture to solve.

× 6	
3	
5	
7	
8	
6	
9	

---

9 in.

4 in.

Multiply the sides to find the area.

_____ × _____ = _____ in.

561	
50	

How many equal groups of 8 are in 48?

2 hours and 20 minutes later:

○ 11: 38 am

○ 11:48 am

○ 11:28 am

32 counters

4 equal groups

_____ counters in each group

$8 \times 2 \times 1 = 1 \times 2 \times 8$

true   **false**

>, <, or =

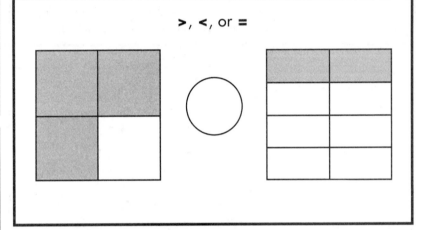

7 × 6	30
8 × 7	64
6 × 8	42
7 × 5	56
7 × 7	49
8 × 8	48
6 × 5	35

$72 \div \underline{\quad} = 8$

54 ÷ 9

The dividend is _____.

The divisor is _____.

The quotient is _____.

Talia has a soccer game at 9:00 am. She lives 20 minutes from the field and needs 40 minutes to eat breakfast and get ready for her game. What time should she wake up to get to her game on time?

Corey plants 25 flowers in 5 equal rows. How many flowers did she plant in each row?

Sasha bought three 2-liter bottles of soda for her party. Her friend brought two more 2 liters. How many liters of soda did the girls have for the party?

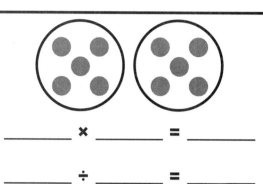

_____ × _____ = _____

_____ ÷ _____ = _____

662

Round to nearest

10: _____

100: _____

445 + 222 = _____

There were 3 birdbaths at the park. Shane counted 4 birds in each bath. Two more birds joined. Then, 3 birds flew away. How many birds were left?

25 ÷ 5	
36 ÷ 6	
28 ÷ 4	
32 ÷ 8	
56 ÷ 7	
48 ÷ 8	
54 ÷ 9	
16 ÷ 4	
21 ÷ 3	
20 ÷ 4	
49 ÷ 7	

Lisa and her mom made tacos for dinner. There are 4 people in their family. Each person ate 2 tacos. How many tacos did the family eat all together? Draw a picture to solve.

_____ × _____ = _____

6 × ☐ = 54

☐ × 9 = 54

54 ÷ ☐ = 6

☐ ÷ 6 = 9

304 − 296 = _____

Solve. Write a story to match.

64 ÷ 8 = _____

_____

_____

_____

_____

Heidi uses 8 inches of string to make a bracelet. How many inches of string does she need to make 4 bracelets? _____ inches

Which is true? ◯ **2 × 1 = 1 + 2**

◯ **1 × 3 = 3 + 1**

◯ **2 × 3 = 3 × 2**

40 ÷ 5	**2**
30 ÷ 5	**4**
15 ÷ 5	**10**
20 ÷ 5	**6**
35 ÷ 5	**8**
45 ÷ 5	**3**
10 ÷ 5	**9**
50 ÷ 5	**7**

6 × 4	**20**
8 × 4	**0**
4 × 4	**24**
10 × 4	**36**
0 × 4	**40**
9 × 4	**32**
5 × 4	**28**
7 × 4	**16**

Coral went for a hike. The hike was 3 hours and 20 minutes long. She started the hike at 8:45 am. What time did she finish the hike? Show your answer on the clock.

Draw a rectangle. Divide it into fourths. Label each fourth.

48 counters

6 equal groups

_____ in each group

6 equal groups

4 in each group

_____ in all

Write an addition sentence to match 4 × 3.

_____ + _____ + _____ = _____

1,000, _____, _____, 880, 840

Sal and his mom baked cookies. They fit 8 cookies on each tray. They made 24 cookies in all. How many trays of cookies did they make?

_____ **trays**

8 ft.

4 ft.

perimeter = ◯ **12 ft.** ◯ **24 ft.** ◯ **32 ft.**

Draw an array to match
20 ÷ 5 = _____.

Owen helps his dad carry in bags of groceries. He carries 3 bags that each hold 4 items, and 1 bag that carries 6 items. How many items does he carry in?

_____ items

$16 \div \boxed{} = 4$

A guitar has 6 strings. How many strings are on

2 guitars? _____

3 guitars? _____

4 guitars? _____

Carly's softball game started at 11:35 am. It lasted one hour and 5 minutes. What time did the game end?

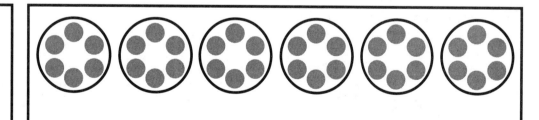

_____ × _____ = _____

Divide into groups to show 12 ÷ 6 = 2.

4⟌28

The dividend is _____.

The divisor is _____.

The quotient is _____.

A roller coaster car can hold 8 people per ride. There are 64 people waiting to ride on the coaster. How many cars will it take to hold all 64 people?

○ **64 + 8**

○ **8 × 64**

○ **64 ÷ 8**

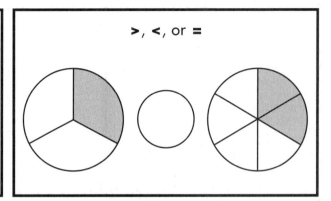

>, <, or =

---

24 campers
3 campers per tent

_____ **tents needed**

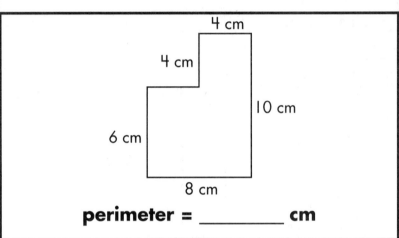

4 cm

4 cm

10 cm

6 cm

8 cm

perimeter = _____ cm

Daryl has 4 packs of 10 stickers. He gives a pack to his sister and 5 stickers to his brother. How many stickers is Daryl left with?

---

7 × 8 = _____

---

42 counters

6 equal groups

_____ counters
in each group

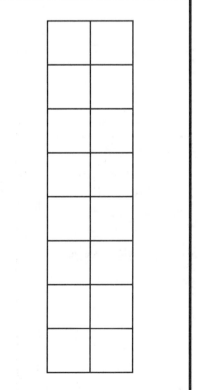

area = _____ sq. units

---

6 × 7 = ☐

7 × 6 = ☐

☐ **÷ 7 = 6**

☐ **÷ 6 = 7**

Which would you use to measure the weight of a dolphin?

grams

kilograms

_____ × _____ = _____

Jim runs 2 miles a day. How many miles does he run in 7 days?

$2 \times (3 \times 2) = 2 \times 6$

true   **false**

Rule:	
15	3
20	4
25	5
30	6
35	7
40	8

× 9	
0	
1	
2	
3	
4	
5	
6	
7	
8	
9	
10	

Troy ate breakfast at 8:08 am. Lunch was 3 hours and 45 minutes later. What time was lunch?

4 shelves

9 books on each shelf

_____ books in all

$42 ÷ \underline{\hspace{1cm}} = 7$

Draw a picture to solve $18 ÷ 3$.

_____ ÷ _____ = _____

$\begin{array}{r} 905 \\ -\ 867 \\ \hline \end{array}$

Jill makes 6 bracelets to give to her friends. Each bracelet uses 9 beads. How many beads does she use in all?

_____ **bracelets** × _____ **beads**

= _____ **beads in all**

× 4	2	4	6	8	10
2					
4					
6					
8					
10					

$18 \div 3 =$ _____

$24 \div 3 =$ _____

$15 \div 3 =$ _____

$9 \div 3 =$ _____

$3 \div 3 =$ _____

$12 \div 3 =$ _____

$0 \div 3 =$ _____

$6 \div 3 =$ _____

$6 \times 4 =$ _____

$3 \times 7 =$ _____

$5 \times 9 =$ _____

$7 \times 7 =$ _____

$6 \times 8 =$ _____

$0 \times 7 =$ _____

$6 \times 7 =$ _____

$7 \times 4 =$ _____

$3 \times 30 =$ _____

$5 \times 30 =$ _____

$6 \times 30 =$ _____

$$\begin{array}{r} 313 \\ 485 \\ +\ 102 \\ \hline \end{array}$$

Emma has 18 cherries. She eats 2. She divides the rest of the cherries evenly into 4 bags. How many cherries are in each bag?

Geo finishes dinner at 6:05 pm. He does homework for 50 minutes and practices guitar for 30 minutes. Then, he watches a 30-minute show on TV. He reads 20 minutes before he gets ready for bed. What time does he start getting ready for bed?

$(6 \times 3) \times 5 = 6 \times ($ _____ × _____ $)$

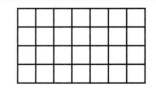

area = _____ **square units**

Zion starts a movie at 6:55 pm. The movie ends at 9:08 pm. How long is the movie?

◯ **2 hours 13 minutes**

◯ **2 hours 10 minutes**

◯ **3 hours 8 minutes**

54 ÷ 6

The dividend is _____.

The divisor is _____.

The quotient is _____.

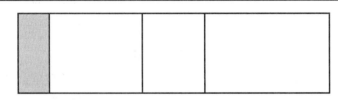

Manuel drew this figure to show one-fourth. Do you agree with his thinking? Why or why not?

_____

_____

_____

_____

33 + 140 is about _____.

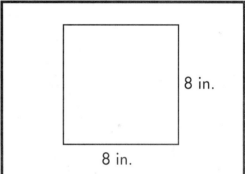

8 in.

8 in.

area = _____ sq. in.

63 ÷ 7	**7**
54 ÷ 6	**7**
56 ÷ 8	**8**
40 ÷ 5	**8**
72 ÷ 9	**9**
81 ÷ 9	**9**
49 ÷ 7	**9**

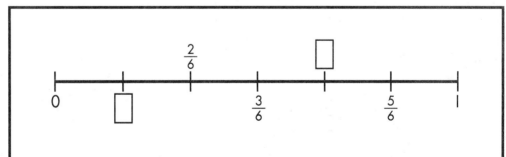

Avery has 4 piles of laundry. Each pile has 6 pieces of clothing. How many pieces of clothing in all?

64 counters

8 equal groups

_____ counters in each group

Trevor jogged 2 miles on Saturday and twice as many miles on Sunday. How many total miles did he jog in both days?

10 cm

8 cm

perimeter = _____ cm

6 cupcakes
2 candles on each cupcake

_____ **candles in all**

Gr. 3	
Gr. 4	
Gr. 5	

Key: = 10 pounds

How many pounds of canned food did third grade collect? _____

How many more pounds did fifth grade collect than third grade? _____

What time is it? _____

What time will it be in 42 minutes? _____

36 ÷ _____ = 4

If 2 × ☐ = 18,

then 18 ÷ ☐ = 2.

☐ = ☐

amount of water in a swimming pool

mL

L

>, <, or =

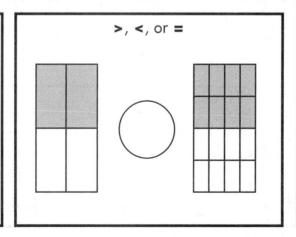

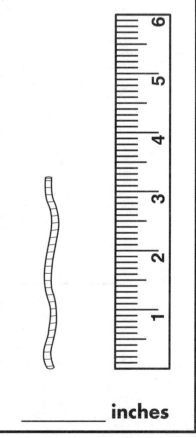

_____ **inches**

Some friends shared 24 cookies equally. Each friend got 4 cookies. How many friends were there in all?

63 in all

7 equal groups

_____ in each group

412 – 209 = _____

What time will it be in 1 hour and 35 minutes?

_____ : _____
am / pm

Color to follow the quotients of 5.

START	
15 ÷ 3	15 ÷ 5
20 ÷ 4	45 ÷ 5
25 ÷ 5	35 ÷ 7
10 ÷ 5	45 ÷ 9
40 ÷ 8	10 ÷ 2
30 ÷ 6	20 ÷ 5
50 ÷ 10	40 ÷ 5
FINISH	

Draw the four different arrays you can make with 8 dots.

I have six sides and six angles. Who am I? Draw me.

929 = about _____ hundreds

16 ÷ 2 = _____
2 × 8 = _____
16 ÷ _____ **= 8**
2 × _____ **= 16**

_____ × _____ = _____

_____ ÷ _____ = _____

152 + 125 is about: ◯ **150 + 120.**

◯ **150 + 125.**

◯ **150 + 130.**

Draw an array to find the product.

6 x 7 = _____

6 x 3 = _____	**24 ÷ 3 = _____**
4 x 4 = _____	**18 ÷ 6 = _____**
6 x 4 = _____	**21 ÷ 7 = _____**
6 x 5 = _____	**32 ÷ 4 = _____**
6 x 6 = _____	**36 ÷ 6 = _____**
5 x 4 = _____	**42 ÷ 7 = _____**
3 x 5 = _____	**48 ÷ 6 = _____**
6 x 8 = _____	**30 ÷ 5 = _____**

20 x 4 = _____

4 x 30 = _____

60 x 3 = _____

56 counters

7 equal groups

_____ in
each group

Jose made trail mix to share with his friends. He put the same amount of ingredients in each bag. Each bag had 5 walnuts, 8 peanuts, 6 raisins, and 7 chocolate chips. He made 5 bags. Find the total number of each ingredient he used.

walnuts _____

peanuts _____

raisins _____

chocolate chips _____

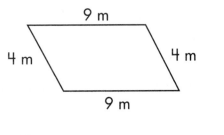

perimeter = _____ m

3 x (_____ x _____) = (3 x 5) x 6

Layla had 15 mL of water in her science beaker. Ian had 43 mL of water. How many more mL did Ian have than Layla?

_____ mL

Staci made 4 groups of 6 counters. Which number sentence can be used to find the total number of counters?

○ 4 + 6 = _____

○ 4 × 6 = _____

○ 6 – 4 = _____

Philippe volunteered at the animal shelter. He fed 8 dogs 3 times in one day. How many bowls of food did he serve that day?

_____ × _____ = _____

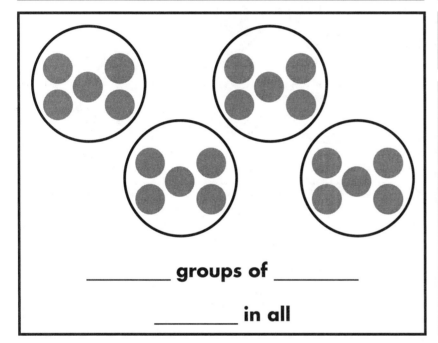

_____ groups of _____

_____ in all

_____ × 6 = 36

Kara collects stickers in a small sticker book. She can fit 8 stickers on each page. How many pages will she need for 40 stickers?

_____ ÷ _____ = _____

24 ÷ 6	8
32 ÷ 4	4
42 ÷ 6	7
48 ÷ 8	6
36 ÷ 4	8
28 ÷ 4	9
64 ÷ 8	7

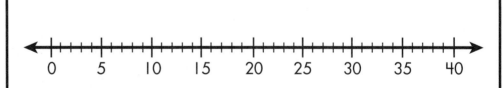

Use the number line to show 5 × 7 = _____.

4 + 4 + 4 = 4 × 3

true   false

42 ÷ 6

The dividend is _____ .

The divisor is _____ .

The quotient is _____ .

Adam had two tomato plants. One plant had 6 tomatoes growing on it, and the other had twice as many. He picked 8 tomatoes. How many were left growing on the plants?

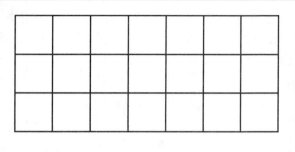

area = _____ square units

45 counters in all

5 equal groups

_____ counters in each group

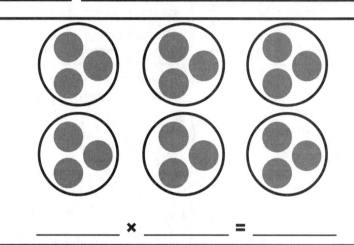

_____ × _____ = _____

Rachel started her homework at 4:33 pm. She worked for 45 minutes and then read for 15 minutes. What time was she done?

_____ : _____ am / pm

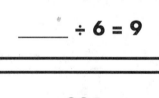 _____ ÷ 6 = 9

```
  336
+ 424
```

4 cm

12 cm   12 cm

4 cm

the mass of a horse

grams

kilograms

Janie had 14 graham crackers. She shared them evenly with her sister. How many graham crackers did each girl get?

perimeter = _____ cm

35 ÷ 5 = _____

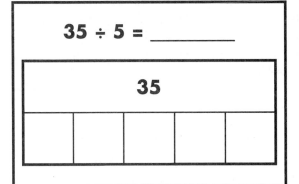

Rosa puts all of her shells into 2 buckets. She puts 9 shells in each bucket. How many shells does she have in all?

154 + 458 = _____

Karyn had two packs of 8 pencils. She sharpened 12 pencils. How many pencils were not sharpened?

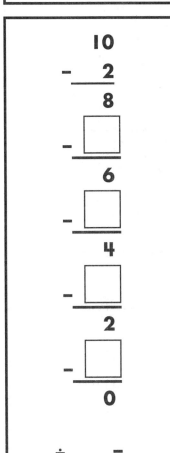

Jeff walks to his friend Marc's house. He leaves his house at 9:15 am. It takes him 12 minutes to walk to Marc's house. He and Marc play basketball for 40 minutes, play a video game for 30 minutes, and then Jeff walks back home. What time does Jeff get home?

_____ : _____

am / pm

A square is labeled 6 cm on each side. What is its perimeter?

_____ cm

306 − 247 = _____

21 counters

3 equal groups

_____ counters in each group

What time is it? _____

What time will it be in 45 minutes? _____

What time was it 45 minutes ago? _____

Four orange slices per friend. Five friends.

◯ 4 + 5

◯ 4 × 5

◯ 4 ÷ 5

Ricki has $25. He buys 4 comic books for $3 each. Then, he buys a new drawing pad for $4. How much money does he have left?

---

12 ÷ 3 = _____

16 ÷ 4 = _____

21 ÷ 7 = _____

24 ÷ 4 = _____

32 ÷ 4 = _____

15 ÷ 3 = _____

40 ÷ 8 = _____

6 × 7 = _____

7 × 0 = _____

3 × 7 = _____

5 × 6 = _____

4 × 6 = _____

8 × 4 = _____

5 × 4 = _____

---

6 × 40 = _____

60 × 5 = _____

7 × 30 = _____

542
+ 301

Draw an array to solve 4 × 7 = _____.

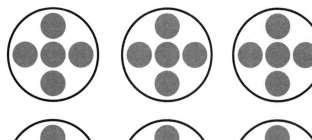

_____ ÷ _____ = _____

503, _____, _____, 563, 583

Each ride at the fair costs 3 tickets. Phoebe has 24 tickets. How many rides can she go on?

Draw a picture to solve 45 ÷ 5 = _____.

Dylan's field hockey team buys jerseys. Each jersey costs $8. If the team spends $72, how many jerseys did they buy?

4 rows of _____ = _____

4 × _____ = _____

_____ **÷ 4 =** _____

177 + 98 is about _____ hundreds.

Eva eats four mini cheeseburgers. Each cheeseburger has 2 pickles on it. How many pickles does she eat in all?

$7\overline{)56}$

$8\overline{)64}$

$4\overline{)36}$

$7\overline{)21}$

$9\overline{)81}$

$6\overline{)54}$

$$\frac{1}{2} = \frac{\square}{4} = \frac{3}{\square} = \frac{\square}{8}$$

(2 × 2) × 4 = 4 × 4

true   false

If 9 × _____ = 54,

then

54 ÷ _____ = _____.

There are 40 prizes in 5 bins. How many prizes are in each bin?

_____ prizes ÷ _____ bins =

_____ prizes in each

There are 10 people on Kurt's baseball team. They each drink 2 bottles of water per game. How many bottles of water do they drink in each game?

$5 \times 2 \times 3 = 3 \times 5 \times 2$

true   **false**

Sanjay has 12 grapes. He eats 2. He gives the rest of the grapes to his friends. Each friend gets 5 grapes. How many friends did Sanjay share with? Show your work.

---

5 cm

6 cm

area = _____ square cm

$42 \div$ _____ $= 6$

$40 \times 4 =$ _____

$60 \times 8 =$ _____

$80 \times 8 =$ _____

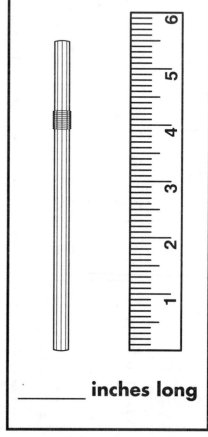

_____ **inches long**

H	T	O
6	0	4
− 4	8	6

Lilly has a lemonade stand. She sells cups of lemonade for $1 each. That morning, 9 people buy lemonade in the first hour, 6 people buy lemonade in the second hour, and 8 people buy lemonade in the third hour. How much money does she make in all?

Break the array to show

_____ ÷ 3 = _____.

---

63 ÷ 9

The dividend is _____.

The divisor is _____.

The quotient is _____.

---

16 ÷ _____ = 4

Hannah counted 4 butterflies in the garden. Mina counted twice as many. How many butterflies did Mina count?

Taj had 4 bags of candy. Each bag held 8 pieces of candy. He gave 4 pieces to his brother and 4 pieces to his sister. How many pieces did Taj have left?

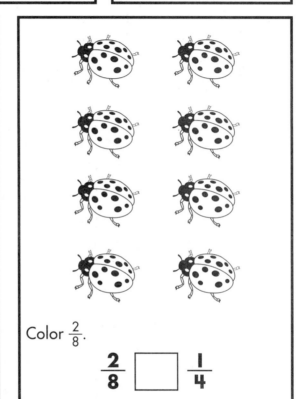

Color $\frac{2}{8}$.

$\frac{2}{8}$ ☐ $\frac{1}{4}$

If 9 × 6 = ☐,

then ☐ ÷ 9 = 6.

☐ = _____

---

8 × _____ = 56

---

5 × 50 = _____

60 × 7 = _____

4 × 80 = _____

A train leaves the station at 8:05 am. Its first stop is 1 hour and 36 minutes away. What time does the train make its first stop? Show your answer on the clock.

472 − 44 is about ◯ **420.**

◯ **430.**

◯ **440.**

Rule: × 8	
2	
4	
6	
8	
10	

the amount of liquid
on a spoon

milliliter

liter

the amount of milk
in a bottle

milliliter

liter

the mass of
a quarter

about 6 g

about 60 kg

the mass of
a female leopard

about 6 g

about 60 kg

$$\begin{array}{r} 122 \\ 25 \\ +\ \underline{192} \end{array}$$

$$\begin{array}{r} 800 \\ -\ \underline{389} \end{array}$$

How many legs on

1 bird? _____

2 birds? _____

3 birds? _____

10 birds? _____

Solve. Color the products with:

2 in the ones place: blue

4 in the ones place: yellow

7 × 2   6 × 9
6 × 7   8 × 4
8 × 9   3 × 4
8 × 3   8 × 8

7, 14, _____, 28, _____, 42

28 counters

4 equal groups

_____ in each group

_____ ÷ _____ = _____

Draw an array to solve 5 × 7 = _____.

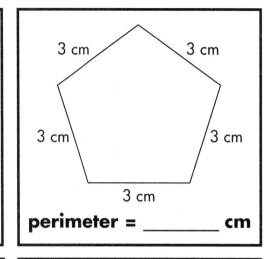

3 cm   3 cm

3 cm   3 cm

3 cm

perimeter = _____ cm

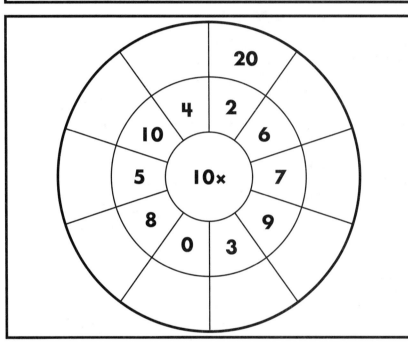

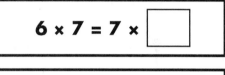

6 × 7 = 7 × ☐

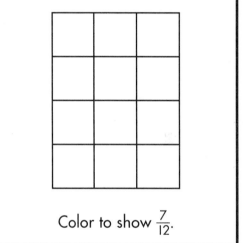

Color to show $\frac{7}{12}$.

÷ 3	
12	
24	
21	
27	
30	
18	

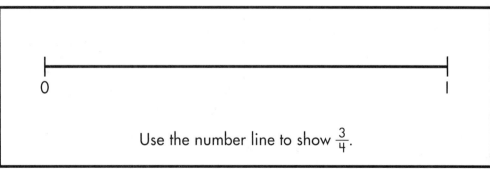

Use the number line to show $\frac{3}{4}$.

802	
	57

48 counters

6 in each group

_____ equal groups

Rafi has 5 packs of peanut butter crackers. Each pack has 4 crackers. How many peanut butter crackers does he have in all?

_____ **×** _____ = _____

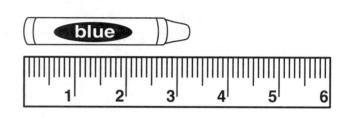

Multiply to find the area.

area = _____ sq. inches

27 counters shared equally

among 3 students.

Each student gets _____ counters.

blue

Measure to the nearest quarter inch.

about _____ inches long

McKenna watches a movie that is 2 hours and 32 minutes long. The movie starts at 11:50 am. What time does the movie end?

_____ : _____
am / pm

16 ÷ _____ = 2

7 groups
7 in each group

_____ **in all**

Ryan had 6 folders in his desk. Each folder held 8 papers. He turned 4 papers in and took 12 papers home. How many papers were left in his desk? Show your work.

A square is labeled 5 cm on one side. What is the perimeter?

perimeter =
_____ **cm**

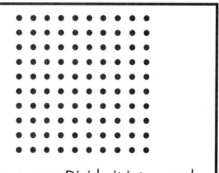

Draw a square. Divide it into equal fourths. Label each fourth.

1,643

Round to nearest

10: _____

100: _____

5 groups

8 in each group

_____ in all

$(1 \times 2) \times 5 = 1 \times (2 + 5)$

true	false

3 × 6	
7 × 3	
6 × 7	
7 × 4	
8 × 6	
6 × 4	
7 × 8	

4 units

10 units   10 units

4 units

area = _____

sq. units

Carlo's family went out for frozen yogurt. They ordered 4 small cups of yogurt, each with 3 different toppings. How many different toppings is that in all? Draw a picture to solve.

$2 \times 8 = 16$

or

$(2 \times 4) + (\underline{\quad} \times 4)$

536 – 488 = _____

mass of a bowling ball

5 grams

5 kilograms

Parallel lines are two lines that never meet and are always the same distance apart. Draw a quadrilateral that has two sets of parallel sides.

Daniella has $24. She spends $6 at lunch. Then, she earns $5 mowing her lawn. How much money does she have now?

An acute angle is less than a 90° right angle. Draw an acute angle.

An obtuse angle is greater than a 90° right angle. Draw an obtuse angle.

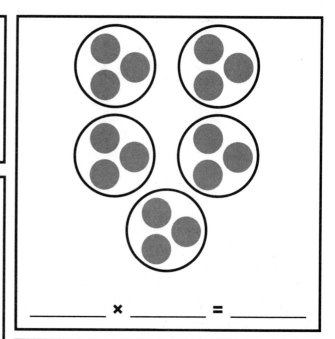

_____ ✗ _____ = _____

8 × 6

_____ rows of 6

_____ in all

7 × 5

_____ rows of 5

_____ in all

Kenya's dance class starts at 5:15 pm. At 6:00, they take a 5-minute break. Then, they dance for 30 more minutes. What time does the class end? Show your answer on the clock.

13 m
9 m   10 m
12 m

perimeter = _____ m

8, _____, 24, _____, 40, _____

Chase puts 32 trading cards into 4 equal groups. How many cards are in each group?

_____ ÷ _____ = _____

□ □ □ □ □ □ □

□ □ □ □ □ □ □

□ □ □ □ □ □ □

□ □ □ □ □ □ □

_____ ÷ _____ = _____

Yvette has 2 baskets of hair accessories. Each basket holds 8 accessories. How many hair accessories does she have in all?

_____ **accessories in all**

Stephan walks 5 minutes to the bus stop. He waits 8 minutes for the bus. He gets on the bus at 11:05 am. What time did he leave his house?

If 8 × 9 = _____,
then _____ ÷ 9 = _____.

Draw a picture to solve
$18 \div 2 =$ _____.

---

6 × 2	
	3 × 6
4 × 4	
	3 × 4
4 × 6	
	6 × 5
5 × 3	

>, <, or =

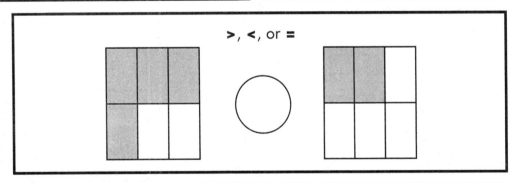

Jeremiah shares raisins equally between himself and 3 friends. Each friend gets 8 raisins. How many raisins were there in all?

_____ × 8 = _____

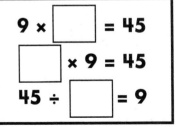

9 × ⬜ = 45

⬜ × 9 = 45

45 ÷ ⬜ = 9

Draw an array to solve 6 x 7 = _____.

area = _____ square units

Rod sees 35 cherries in 5 bowls. How many cherries in each bowl?

_____ ÷ _____ = _____

Kristina makes triangles out of toothpicks. She uses one toothpick for each side of the triangle. How many triangles can she make with 12 toothpicks? Draw a picture and write a number sentence to solve.

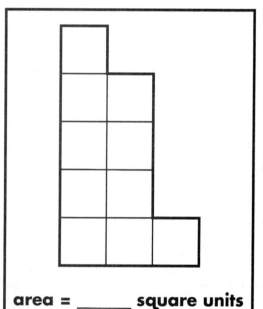

area = _____ square units

30 ÷ ☐ = 5

Twenty-four counters shared equally with 4 friends equals _____ counters per friend.

× 3	
40	
60	
30	
80	
70	
90	
20	
50	
10	

Cam walks his dog 3 miles every week. How many miles do they walk in 4 weeks?

_____ miles

Jenna has 4 packs of crayons. There are 8 crayons in each pack. She gives her brother one whole pack and her little sister 4 crayons. How many crayons does she have left?

Start time: 2:50 pm

Elapsed time: 3 hours and 25 minutes

End time: _____:_____

am/pm

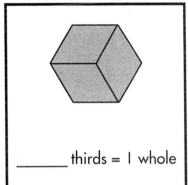

_____ thirds = 1 whole

If 6 × 7 = ⬜ ,

then ⬜ ÷ 6 = 7.

Jim has 2 dogs. He gives each dog 2 treats a day. How many treats does he feed his dogs in 7 days?

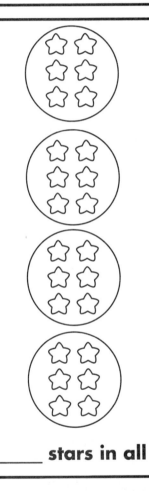

_____ **stars in all**

Tori has a bookcase in her room. The bookcase has 4 shelves. Three of the shelves hold 10 books each, and the other shelf holds 5 books. How many books are on the bookcase? Show your work.

16 in all

4 equal groups

_____ in each group

_____ × 9 = 27

4 groups

5 in each group

_____ in all

Draw a picture to solve 24 ÷ 6= _____.

Kennedy read 9 pages in her book every day in one week. How many pages did she read in all?

12	24	4	6
15	3	5	3
5	8	4	2
3	3	1	0

Circle the division facts.

_____ × _____

= _____

$36 \div 6 =$ _____

$24 \div 6 =$ _____

$18 \div 6 =$ _____

$12 \div 6 =$ _____

$42 \div 6 =$ _____

$6 \div 6 =$ _____

$30 \div 6 =$ _____

45 in all

5 groups

_____ in each

48 in all

6 groups

_____ in each

Millie shared a whole small pizza with some friends. They each ate $\frac{1}{4}$ of the pizza. How many friends ate the pizza?

Draw lines from the center number to the problems that match it.

2 × 2   24 ÷ 6   24 ÷ 8

1 × 4   (4)   20 ÷ 5

32 ÷ 4   16 ÷ 4   20 ÷ 4

6, 12, 18, _____, _____, _____

area = _____ square units

_____ ÷ _____ = _____

Lila used 3 purple beads for each necklace. She made six necklaces. How many purple beads did she use in all?

Soccer practice started at 5:45 pm. It lasted 1 hour and 40 minutes. What time did it end?

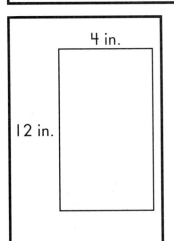

503 + 356 = _____

Niko builds 4 towers. Each tower is made of 8 cubes. He builds another tower that is made of 12 cubes. How many cubes does he use in all?

4 in.

12 in.

perimeter =

_____ in.

Divide the number line into fifths. Label each point.

0 ———————————————————— 1

$4 \times 6 = 4 \times (3 + 3)$

true   **false**

700
− 584
———

678 + 203 is about ◯ **800.**

◯ **880.**

◯ **900.**

Circle the parallel sides. Name the polygon.

_____

874 is about _____ hundreds

Travis goes for a hike with his dad. They start their hike at 8:45 am and hike for 1 hour and 15 minutes. Then, they take a 20-minute rest before hiking back. They hike back down for 1 hour and 15 minutes. What time is it when they complete their hike?

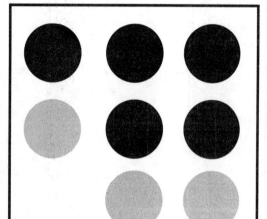

fraction of black = _____

fraction of gray = _____

9 × 6 = _____

63 in all

7 equal groups

_____ in each group

÷ 8	
8	
24	
64	
16	
32	
24	
72	
80	

Show $\frac{6}{8}$.

4 units

3 units

area = _____ square units

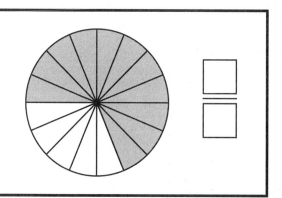

The perimeter of a square is 16 in. What is the length of each side?

224 – 148 = _____

Lyn sold 22 raffle tickets on Saturday and 37 tickets on Sunday. About how many tickets did she sell in both days?

Kelli bought a bouquet of 12 flowers. Half of them are red. The other half are yellow. How many of the flowers are red?

Greg found 81 paper clips in his dad's office. Half of them are red. He divided them equally into 9 boxes. How many were in each box?

5 cm

9 cm

area = _____ **×** _____

= _____ **square cm**

Four books of 20 stamps equals

_____ stamps in all.

24 ÷ _____ = 6

56 counters

7 groups

_____ in each group

Favorite Fruits

	1	2	3	4	5	6
apples						
bananas						
strawberries						
peaches						

Number of Students

Which fruit had the most votes? _____

Which fruit had the least votes? _____

How many more students chose peaches than apples? _____

_____ ÷ _____ = _____

The clock shows what time the movie ended. The movie lasted 2 hours and 20 minutes. What time did it start?

× 7	
4	
3	
6	
0	
2	
9	
1	
10	
8	

÷ 7	
56	
14	
42	
35	
7	
14	
70	
63	
21	

4 × 7

_____ rows of 7

_____ in all

a glass of water

milliliters

liters

Carmen brought four tins of cookies to the party. Each tin held 8 cookies. At the end of the party, there were only 3 cookies left. How many cookies were eaten at the party?

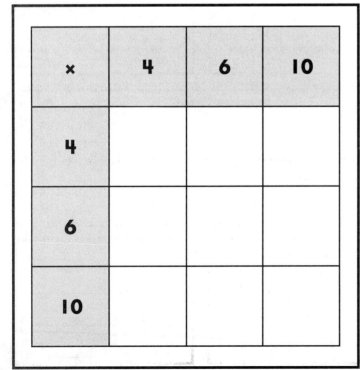

×	4	6	10
4			
6			
10			

635, 665, _____, _____, _____

Kaden scored 225 points on Level 1 of a video game. He scored 340 points on Level 2. How many points did he score in all?

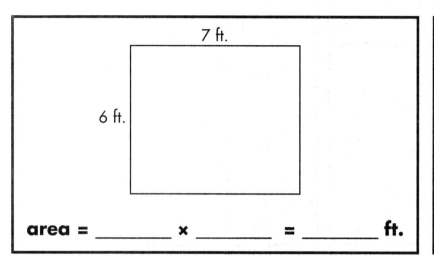

area = _____ **×** _____ = _____ **ft.**

There are 104 fiction books in the class library and 89 nonfiction books. About how many more fiction books than nonfiction?

Color odd quotients yellow and even quotients blue.

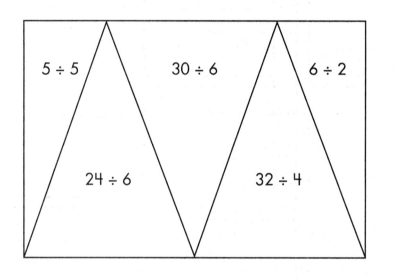

$5 \div 5$
$30 \div 6$
$6 \div 2$
$24 \div 6$
$32 \div 4$

400 – 123 = _____

Marie paints 4 paintings. She uses 3 different colors in each painting. How many different colors does she use in all?

9 × 4 = _____

5 × 7 = _____

0 × 1 = _____

4 × 6 = _____

6 × 9 = _____

7 × 6 = _____

5 × 8 = _____

Breanna walked $\frac{5}{8}$ of a mile. Which point represents the distance she walked?

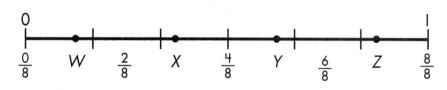

Jesse has $45. He buys 2 games online for $10 each, plus $3 shipping for the whole order. How much money does he have left?

32 counters

4 rows

_____ in each row

Start time: 9:05 am

Elapsed time: 4 hours 23 minutes

End time: _____:_____

am/pm

Beaker A holds 53 mL. Beaker B holds 34 mL. How many more mL does Beaker A hold than Beaker B?

_____ mL

---

7 rows

7 circles in each row

_____ circles in all

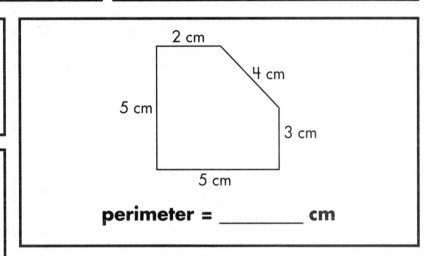

perimeter = _____ cm

A bag of candy has more than 40 but less than 60 pieces. The number of candy has an 8 in the ones place. The candy can be divided evenly by 6. How many candies are in the bag?

---

16 ÷ _____ = 8

429
− 358

Follow the answers of 4.

START	
35 ÷ 7	24 ÷ 6
40 ÷ 8	12 − 8
12 ÷ 3	2 × 2
4 × 1	4 × 2
40 ÷ 10	8 ÷ 4
6 − 2	32 ÷ 8
12 − 6	8 − 4
FINISH	

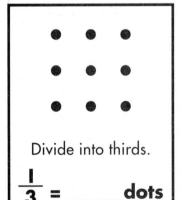

Divide into thirds.

$\frac{1}{3}$ = _____ **dots**

>, <, or =

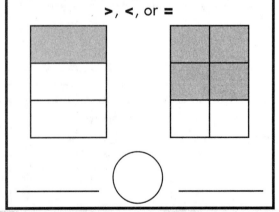

_____ ◯ _____

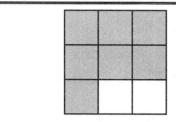

shaded parts =

○ **9/9**   ○ **7/9**   ○ **2/9**

457 – 234 rounded to nearest tens is about

4 × 5 = 5 × 4

true   **false**

more than one liter

about one liter

less than one liter

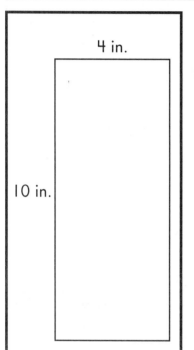

4 in.

10 in.

area = _____ sq. in.

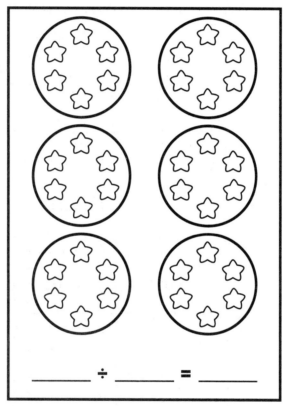

_____ ÷ _____ = _____

Meg arrived at the game 34 minutes before it started. The game started at 8:00 am. What time did she get to the game?

_____ : _____

114 + 588 = _____

54 counters

6 equal groups

_____ in each group

_____ ÷ _____ = _____

Elapsed time: 3 hours 15 minutes

Start time: 2:30 pm

End time: _____

Jairo walks some dogs in his neighborhood. He gets paid $2 per dog for each walk. He walks 3 dogs twice a day. How much money can he make in one day?

Draw lines to match.

48 ÷ 8	**4**
32 ÷ 4	**5**
54 ÷ 6	**6**
18 ÷ 2	**7**
16 ÷ 4	**7**
25 ÷ 5	**8**
21 ÷ 3	**9**
49 ÷ 7	**9**

3 × ☐ = 18

☐ × 3 = 21

4 × 7 = ☐

6 × ☐ = 24

☐ × 4 = 32

8 × 3 = ☐

Start time: 9:15 am

Elapsed time: 4 hours 15 minutes

Show the end time on the clock.

There are 8 dogs at the dog park. Each dog has 2 tags on its collar. How many tags are there in all?

Eight students share 24 counters. How many per student?

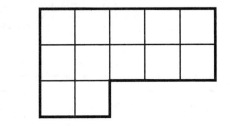

perimeter = _____ units

9, 18, 27, _____, _____,

_____, _____, _____,

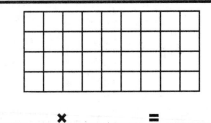

_____ × _____ = _____

Draw a picture to solve 42 ÷ 7 = _____.

>, <, or =

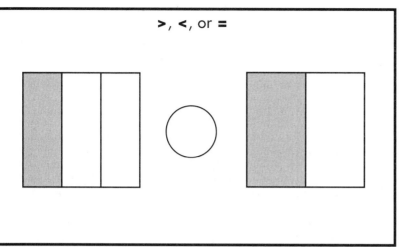

Granola bars are sold in boxes of 8. Ms. Lincoln has 24 students in her class. How many boxes of granola bars should she buy to make sure she has enough for each student to have one?

Celine sold cupcakes at the bake sale. In the morning, she sold 23 cupcakes. In the afternoon, she sold 22 cupcakes. At the end of the day, she was left with 3 cupcakes. How many cupcakes did she bring to the bake sale?

150 – _____ = 50

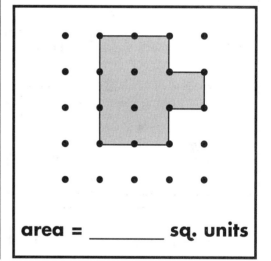

area = _____ sq. units

Draw lines to match.

2 × 6   3 × 6

5 × 3   6 × 2

6 × 3   4 × 6

3 × 4   3 × 5

6 × 4   4 × 3

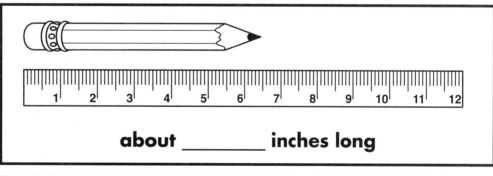

about _____ inches long

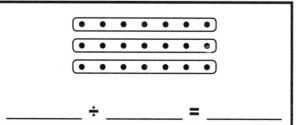

_____ ÷ _____ = _____

36 counters in all

4 equal rows

_____ in each row

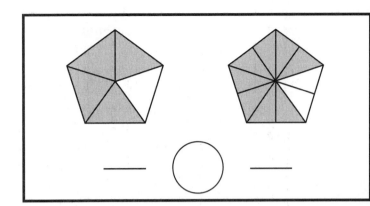

_____ ◯ _____

_____ × _____ = _____

Seventy-two pennies are divided evenly between 8 students equals _____ pennies for each student.

A hexagon has _____ sides and _____ angles. Circle the hexagons.

Ben´s mom bought 3 packs of yogurt. Each pack contained 4 yogurts. Ben ate 2 yogurts and his sister ate 1 yogurt. How many yogurts are left?

$32 \div 4 =$ _____

```
  201
-  99
```

Gregg drew a polygon that had one side less than a hexagon. What did he draw?

_____

Draw an example.

```
  147
  423
+ 240
```

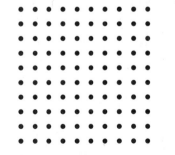

Draw a rectangle. Divide it into 5 equal parts and label.

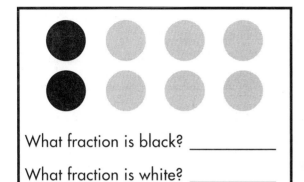

What fraction is black? _____

What fraction is white? _____

4 groups

7 in each

_____ **in all**

If 6 × ☐ = 48,

then 48 ÷ 6 = ☐ .

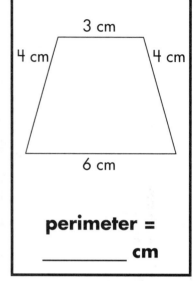

perimeter = _____ **cm**

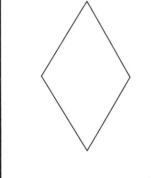

Circle all that apply.

rhombus

quadrilateral

rectangle

parallelogram

Kate made 4 pizzas. She cut each pizza into 6 slices. How many slices of pizza did she make? Draw a picture to solve.

_____ **slices in all**

line segment

true   false

35 ÷ _____ = 5

56 counters

7 groups

_____ in each group

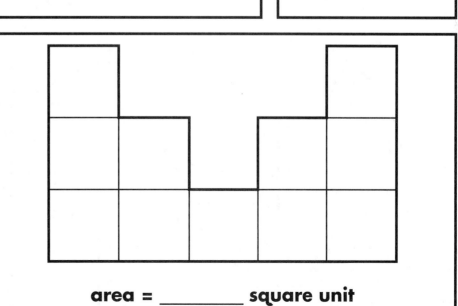

area = _____ square unit

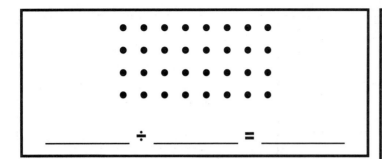

_____ ÷ _____ = _____

÷ 6	
24	
48	
12	
72	
30	
36	

÷ 8	
16	
40	
48	
24	
64	
32	

Divide to show sixths. Label each part.

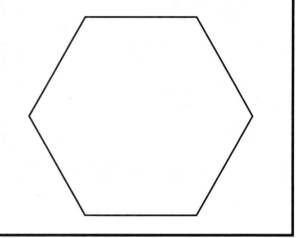

```
  654
+ 289
```

60 × 7 = _____

70 × 8 = _____

80 × 9 = _____

Morgan started karate class at 6:05 pm. Class lasted one hour and 45 minutes. What time did class end?

The Lewis family drove 215 miles on the first day of their trip. On the second day, they drove 378 miles. About how many miles did they drive in all?

_____ + _____ is about _____.

615, 600, _____, _____, 555

```
 0   1   2   3   4   5   6
 6   6   6   6   6   6   6
```

>, <, or =

$\frac{2}{6}$ ◯ $\frac{4}{6}$

Solve and write a story for **32 ÷ 4** = _____ .

_____

_____

_____

_____

---

6 m

4 m

area = _____ **×** _____

= _____ **square m**

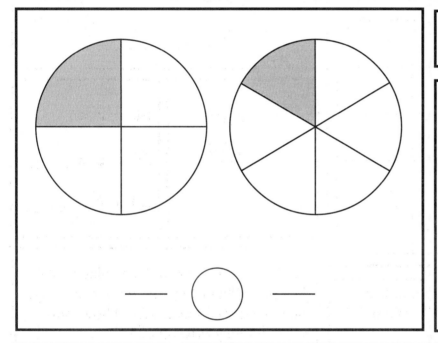

___ ◯ ___

---

482 is about
_____ hundreds.

Jonah is saving for a video game that costs $45. He has $22. Then, he earns $6 for his allowance, and $10 for babysitting. How much more money does he need to pay for the video game?

---

9 × 7	
6 × 7	
7 × 8	
8 × 6	
9 × 8	
7 × 7	
6 × 9	

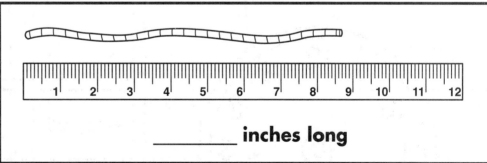

_____ **inches long**

Annie bought 12 new books. Half of them were fiction. The other half were nonfiction. How many of the books were nonfiction?

Eight students share 48 crayons. How many crayons does each student get?

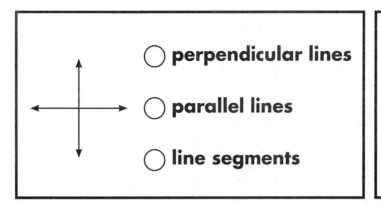

○ perpendicular lines

○ parallel lines

○ line segments

>, <, or =

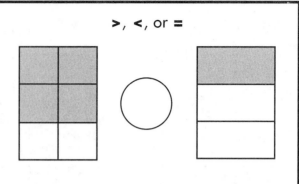

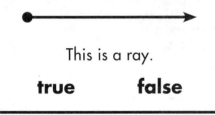

This is a ray.

true   **false**

Val went to volunteer at the hospital at 3:10 pm. He got home 4 hours and 33 minutes later. What time did he get home?

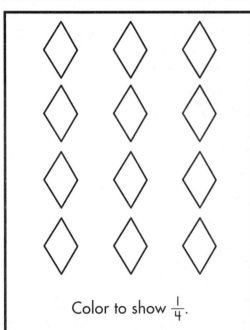

Color to show $\frac{1}{4}$.

8 × _____ = 72

Nine students share 45 counters. How many does each student get?

27
573
+ 228

Nick's little brother has 6 toy cars. $\frac{2}{6}$ of the cars are red. The rest are blue. What fraction of the cars are blue?

Follow the path of the odd quotients.

START	
54 ÷ 6	42 ÷ 7
81 ÷ 9	24 ÷ 3
56 ÷ 8	49 ÷ 7
48 ÷ 6	30 ÷ 6
10 ÷ 5	15 ÷ 3
12 ÷ 4	27 ÷ 9
25 ÷ 5	24 ÷ 6
6 ÷ 6	30 ÷ 3
FINISH	

Start time: 1:20 pm

Elapsed time: 3 hours 15 minutes

End time: _____ : _____

Draw a pair of parallel lines.

$7 \times 2 =$ _____ $\times 7$

5 cm

8 cm

area = _____ **cm**

Find the area of each rectangle. Add to find the area of the whole shape.

4 ft.

8 ft.

4 ft.

_____ + _____

area = _____ **ft.**

weight of a butterfly

grams

kilograms

_____ **cubes**

$36 \div$ _____ $= 6$

27 cubes

3 rows

_____ in each row

Pam measured pieces of string to the nearest quarter inch:
$4\frac{1}{2}$, $4\frac{1}{4}$, $4\frac{1}{2}$, $4\frac{3}{4}$, $4\frac{1}{4}$, 5, $5\frac{1}{4}$, $4\frac{1}{4}$, $4\frac{1}{2}$, $5\frac{1}{4}$, and $4\frac{3}{4}$.
Fill in the data on the line plot. The first one is plotted for you.

Lengths of Strings

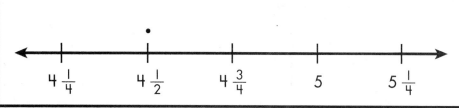

$4\frac{1}{4}$ $4\frac{1}{2}$ $4\frac{3}{4}$ 5 $5\frac{1}{4}$

Start time: 11:40 am

End time: 2:10 pm

Elapsed time: _____ hours _____ minutes

6 × 6	
5 × 8	
3 × 0	
7 × 4	
6 × 7	
7 × 8	

63 ÷ 9	
54 ÷ 6	
28 ÷ 7	
36 ÷ 4	
42 ÷ 7	
48 ÷ 6	

Sam played a game with his sister. He scored 4 points in the first round and lost 2 points in the second round. Then, he gained 5 points in the last round. How many points did he end up with?

_____ **points**

4 rows

4 in each row

_____ in all

36 in all

9 in each row

_____ rows

Harry's mom packed 4 lunch bags for a picnic. Each bag had 1 sandwich, 2 fruits, and 1 drink. How many

sandwiches? _____

fruits? _____

drinks? _____

$3 \times 14 = (3 \times 7) + (3 \times 7)$

true   **false**

1

$\frac{1}{8}$	$\frac{1}{8}$	$\frac{1}{8}$	$\frac{1}{8}$	$\frac{1}{8}$	$\frac{1}{8}$	$\frac{1}{8}$	$\frac{1}{8}$

$\frac{1}{3}$	$\frac{1}{3}$	$\frac{1}{3}$

$\frac{4}{8}$ ◯ $\frac{2}{3}$

Number line: 0, $\frac{1}{8}$, □, $\frac{3}{8}$, □, $\frac{5}{8}$, □, $\frac{7}{8}$, 1 with $\frac{1}{4}$, $\frac{2}{4}$, $\frac{3}{4}$ marked above

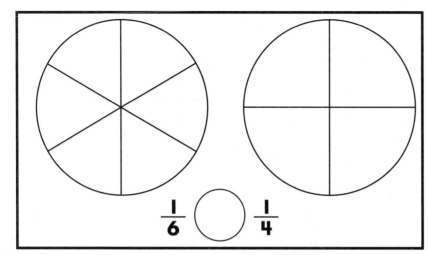

$\frac{1}{6}$ ◯ $\frac{1}{4}$

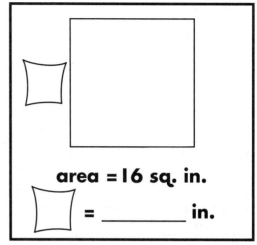

area = 16 sq. in.

= _____ in.

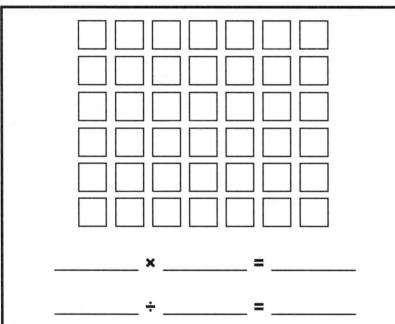

_____ × _____ = _____

_____ ÷ _____ = _____

632 + 205 = _____

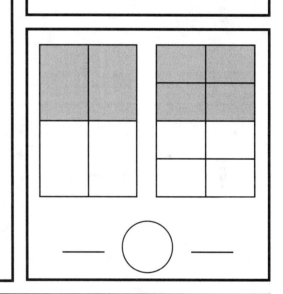

_____ ◯ _____

A tricycle has 3 wheels. How many wheels on

2? _____

4? _____

6? _____

8? _____

Isaac had 4 packs of colored pencils. Each pack had the same amount of pencils in it. He gave 2 pencils to his sister. He now has 30 colored pencils. How many pencils were in each pack?

Antonia has 48 seeds. She plants 6 seeds in each planter. How many planters does she fill?

8 teams

56 players

_____ on each team

3 × 16 = 3 × (8 + 8)

    = (3 × _____) + (3 × _____)

    = _____ + _____

    = _____

Start time: 4:18 pm

Elapsed time: 2 hours 22 minutes

End time: _____

42 candies. 6 friends.

_____ candies for each friend.

_____ ÷ _____ = _____

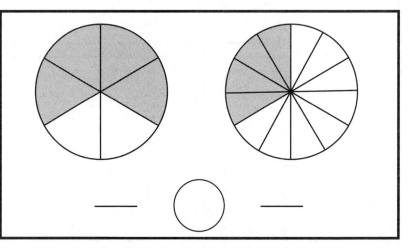

____ ◯ ____

4 cm

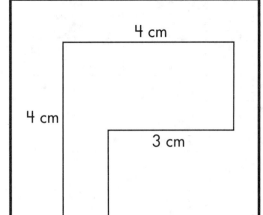

4 cm

3 cm

1 cm

perimeter = _____ cm

500 – 175 = _____

18 stars

2 in each row

_____ rows

mount of juice
in a juice box

mL

L

Draw a polygon with one pair of
parallel sides and two right angles.

8 × 7 =	
6 × 9 =	
9 × 8 =	
6 × 8 =	
7 × 6 =	
0 × 9 =	
8 × 4 =	
7 × 7 =	

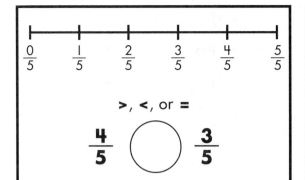

>, <, or =

$\frac{4}{5}$ ◯ $\frac{3}{5}$

48 shells

6 piles

_____ in each pile

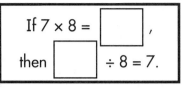

If $7 \times 8 =$ ☐ ,

then ☐ $\div 8 = 7$.

The fraction of boys in the Martinson family is $\frac{3}{5}$. How many girls are in the family?

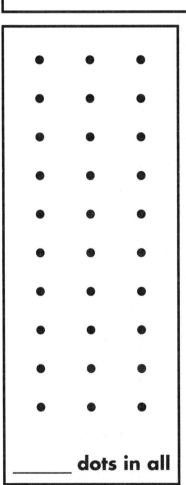

_____ dots in all

210 – 86 = _____

425 + 178 is about

_____ + _____

or 600.

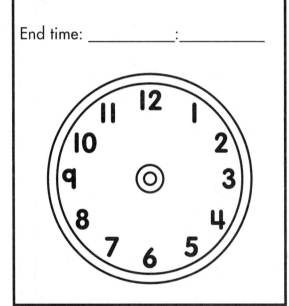

Start time: 8:48 am

Elapsed time: 4 hours, 15 minutes

End time: _____:_____

3 rows

_____ in each row

27 in all

_____ ÷ _____ = _____

Lengths of sticks in inches are $5\frac{1}{2}$, 6, $6\frac{1}{2}$, $6\frac{1}{4}$, $5\frac{3}{4}$, $5\frac{1}{4}$, $5\frac{1}{4}$, $6\frac{1}{2}$, $5\frac{1}{2}$, $6\frac{1}{4}$, $6\frac{1}{4}$, $5\frac{3}{4}$, and 5. Use the data to create a line plot.

Lengths of Sticks

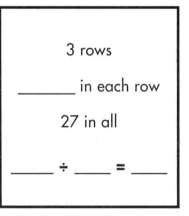

| 5 | $5\frac{1}{4}$ | $5\frac{1}{2}$ | $5\frac{3}{4}$ | 6 | $6\frac{1}{4}$ | $6\frac{1}{2}$ |

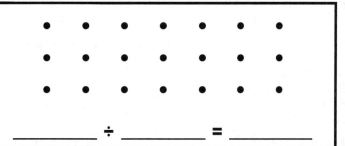

_____ ÷ _____ = _____

Rule: × 7	
3	
5	
8	
4	
7	
9	

Rule: ÷ 3	
24	
15	
21	
3	
12	
30	

28	48	8	6
4	2	6	24
7	32	4	8
5	27	9	3

Circle the division facts.

Draw an acute angle.

Draw an obtuse angle.

>, <, or =

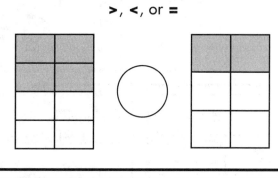

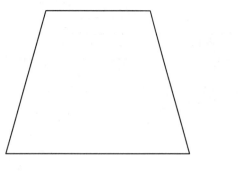

Name the polygon. _____

Trace the parallel sides in red.

Trace the intersecting sides in blue.

Raquel buys 3 packs of hair bands. Each pack has 4 bands. She gives 3 bands to her sister. How many hair bands does she have left?

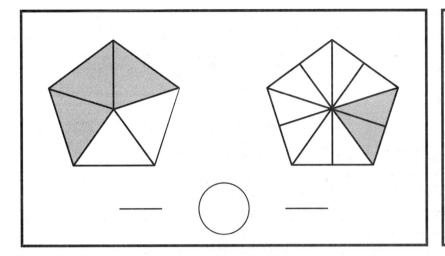

_____ ◯ _____

Shay went to bed at 9:05 pm. She woke up at 6:45 am. How long did she sleep?

_____ **hours and**

_____ **minutes**

red	👕👕
blue	👕👕👕👕👕👕
white	👕👕👕👕👕
green	👕👕👕

Key: 👕 = 3 shirts

How many green shirts does the store have on sale?

_____

How many more blue shirts than red shirts? _____

How many fewer white shirts than blue? _____

444 + 288 = _____

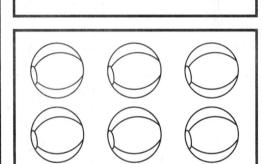

Color to show $\frac{1}{3}$.

× 8	
3	
4	
5	
6	
7	
8	

Gaby has 5 packs of markers. Each pack holds 6 markers. She gives one pack to a friend. Then, she shares the remaining markers between herself and 3 other friends. How many markers does each girl get?

9 ft.

4 ft.   4 ft.

9 ft.

perimeter = _____ ft.

weight of laptop

grams

kilograms

427 − 176 is about ◯ **420 − 180.**

◯ **430 − 170.**

◯ **430 − 180.**

Color to show $\frac{4}{6} > \frac{3}{6}$.

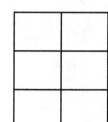 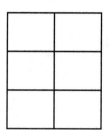

If 9 × 7 = ☐ ,

then ☐ ÷ 9 = 7.

4 × 16 = 4 × (8 + 8)

= (4 × _____) + (4 × _____)

= _____ + _____

= _____

A   B

ray AB

line segment AB

line AB

24 ÷ _____ = 3

Circle the right angles.

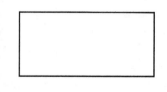

6 × 8	
48 ÷ 6	
7 × 6	
42 ÷ 7	
8 × 8	
64 ÷ 8	
7 × 8	
56 ÷ 7	

16 counters

4 are red

fraction of red =

_____

Caroline counted 48 pencils. The pencils were in packs of 8. How many packs were there?

Name _____

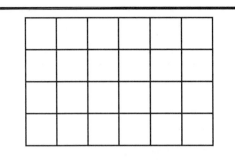

area = _____ square units

Color to show $\frac{1}{4}$.

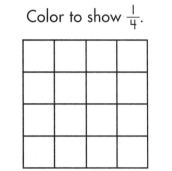

If $9 \times 5 =$ _____,

then _____ $\div 5 = 9$.

>, <, or =

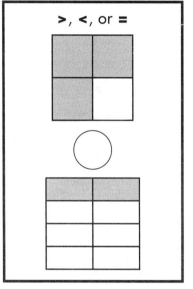

5 × 4	
1 × 0	
6 × 3	
4 × 7	
6 × 4	
0 × 0	
1 × 10	
6 × 6	
7 × 6	
4 × 10	

David leaves the airport at 3:18 pm. It takes him 2 hours and 24 minutes to get home. What time does he get home from the airport?

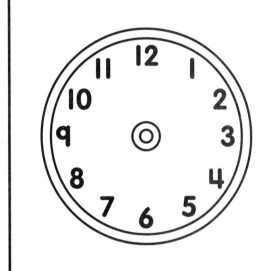

Thirty-two grapes are shared by 4 kids. How many grapes does each kid eat?

302 + 288 = _____

The perimeter of a square is 24 cm. What is the length of each side?

Todd measured the lengths of inchworms in inches: $\frac{3}{4}$, $1\frac{1}{2}$, $\frac{1}{2}$, $1\frac{1}{2}$, $1\frac{1}{4}$, $\frac{3}{4}$, $\frac{3}{4}$, $1\frac{1}{2}$, 2, $1\frac{1}{4}$, $\frac{1}{2}$, and $1\frac{3}{4}$. Use the data to create a line plot.

Lengths of inchworms

```
    |----|----|----|----|----|----|----|----|
    0    1/4  1/2  3/4   1   1 1/4 1 1/2 1 3/4  2
```

141

The Taylor family ordered 4 pizzas for their party. Each pizza was cut into 8 slices. How many slices of pizza did they have in all?

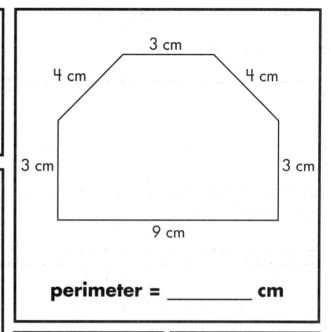

perimeter = _____ cm

Rule: ÷ 4	
24	
40	
12	
·20	
32	

Rule: ÷ 6	
12	
18	
24	
30	
6	

28 in all

1 in each row

_____ rows

63 in all

63 rows

_____ in each row

Wayne bought 3 packs of T-shirts for basketball practice. He gave 3 T-shirts to his teammates. Now, Wayne has 15 T-shirts. How many T-shirts were in each pack?

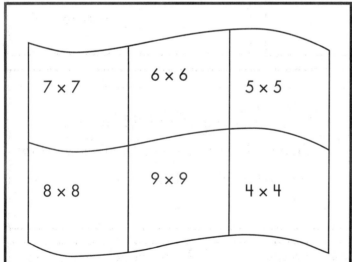

Solve. Color the spaces with even products yellow. Color the spaces with odd products green.

300, 325, _____, _____, 400, _____

End time: 4:50 pm

Elapsed time: 2 hours and 15 minutes

Start time: _____ : _____ **am/pm**

Divide the number line into eighths. Plot and label all points from 0 to 1.

|————————————————————————|

Horatio has 4 packs of fruit snacks. Each pack had 8 snacks in it. He gave 1 pack to his brother, and ate 1 pack. How many fruit snacks does he have left?

>, <, or =

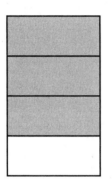   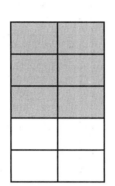

636 is about _____ hundreds.

Kandi's family goes for a 2-mile walk each night. If they walk 4 nights in a week, how many miles do they walk each week?

_____ **miles**

15÷3	
16÷2	
16÷4	
18÷2	
18÷3	
18÷6	
16÷8	

Kora got to the mall at 1:28 pm. She shopped for 3 hours and 15 minutes. What time did she finish shopping?

The daycare had 24 toys stored in 4 bins. How many toys in each bin?

backpack with books

grams

kilograms

7 in.

3 in.

area = _____ square inches

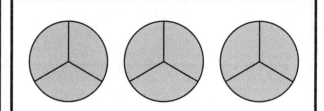

3 wholes = _____ thirds

>, <, or =

$\dfrac{1}{5}$ ◯ $\dfrac{4}{5}$

Rob helps his dad cook dinner. He estimates that a pot of soup holds about 1,000 liters. Is that a good estimate? Why or why not?

_____

_____

_____

2	**× 6 =**	
4	**× 6 =**	
6	**× 6 =**	
8	**× 6 =**	
10	**× 6 =**	

_____ ÷ 8 = 9

64 in all

8 rows

_____ in each row

Circle all the words that describe the polygon.

quadrilateral

rectangle

square

parallelogram

48
552
+ 264

Draw a pair of intersecting lines.

Divide the square into 8 equal parts.
Label each part as a fraction.

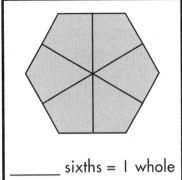

_____ sixths = 1 whole

700 – 478 = _____

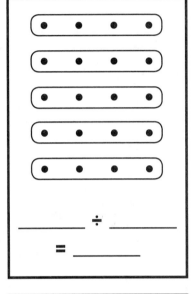

_____ ÷ _____

= _____

_____ **inches**

Start time: 7:35 am

Elapsed time: 6 hours 14 minutes

End time: _____ : _____ **am/pm**

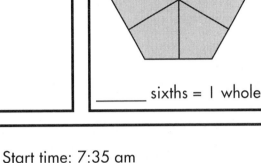

72 counters

_____ rows

8 in each row

Draw a picture to solve 18 ÷ 6 = _____.

_____ **÷ 6 = 7**

40 × 9 = _____

50 × 9 = _____

60 × 9 = _____

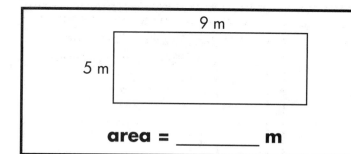

area = _____ m

Rule × 7	
4	
	21
6	
	35
2	
	49

Rule ÷ 2	
8	
	4
16	
	10
14	
	6

Draw a picture to solve:

$\dfrac{1}{4} = \dfrac{\square}{8}$

21 in all

7 in each row

_____ rows

6 groups

7 in each group

_____ in all

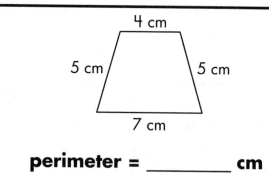

perimeter = _____ cm

271, 311, _____, 391, _____

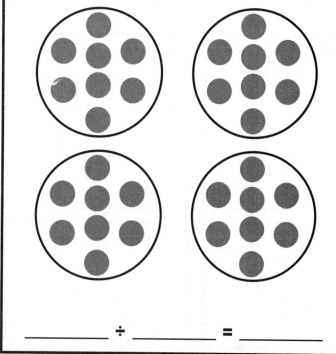

_____ ÷ _____ = _____

$\dfrac{12}{3} =$ _____

A movie started at 7:50 pm. It lasted 2 hours and 42 minutes. What time did it end?

○ **10:22 pm**

○ **10:26 pm**

○ **10:32 pm**

Lauryn had 120 mL of vinegar in her science beaker. Kent had 137 mL. Who had more? How much more?

>, <, or =

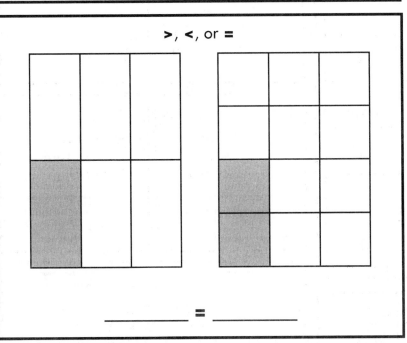

_____ = _____

$8 \times 9 = $ _____ $\times 8$

Sheryl counted 30 dimes in her piggy bank. If 10 dimes make one dollar, how many dollars did she have?

Rule: ÷ 4	
24	
16	
	8
	9
40	
20	

area = _____ square units

$1 \times 2 \times 7 = 7 + 2 + 1$

true   **false**

Draw a line segment.

Which quadrilateral has only one pair of parallel sides?

○ **rhombus**

○ **trapezoid**

○ **rectangle**

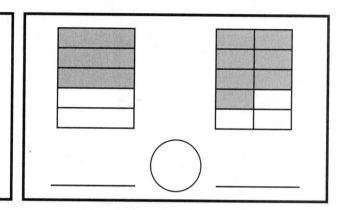

_____   ◯   _____

$4 \times (4 \times 5) = (4 \times 4) \times 5$

true   **false**

Summer Travels

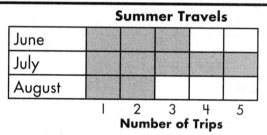

In which month were the most trips taken? _____
In which month were the least trips taken? _____
How many more trips were taken in July than August?
_____

Isla packed 2 small coolers for the beach. Each cooler held 6 bottles of water. She gave 6 bottles of water to her friends and drank 2 bottles herself. How many bottles did she have left?

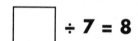 **÷ 7 = 8**

Thirty-six counters shared equally among 4 students is _____ counters per student.

Follow the path of the even quotients.

START	
36 ÷ 6	40 ÷ 5
27 ÷ 9	56 ÷ 7
42 ÷ 7	18 ÷ 3
48 ÷ 6	30 ÷ 6
32 ÷ 8	25 ÷ 5
16 ÷ 4	21 ÷ 3
24 ÷ 3	64 ÷ 8
35 ÷ 5	20 ÷ 10
FINISH	

---

a paper napkin

grams

kilograms

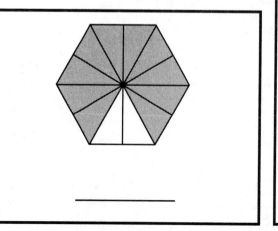

_____

• • • • • •
• • • • • •
• • • • • •
• • • • • •

_____ × _____ = _____

$6 \times 70 =$ _____

$8 \times 90 =$ _____

$5 \times 60 =$ _____

$9 \times 50 =$ _____

$304 - 158 =$ _____

Four friends share 2 packs of stickers. Each pack contains 12 stickers. How many stickers does each friend get?

$18 \div 3$	
$16 \div 4$	
$24 \div 4$	
$21 \div 3$	
$28 \div 7$	
$32 \div 8$	
$48 \div 6$	
$42 \div 7$	

Start time: 11:42 am

Elapsed time: 3 hours 34 minutes

End time: _____ : _____ **am/pm**

16 rows

8 in each row

_____ rows in all

$49 \div$ _____ $= 7$

Draw a picture to solve $36 \div 9 =$ _____.

632 + 278 is about 800.

true   **false**

The Simmons family rents 3 movies each month. In how many months did they watch 24 movies?

6 × 4	21	27 ÷ 3	9
7 × 3	18	24 ÷ 8	9
4 × 8	24	36 ÷ 9	3
6 × 8	28	32 ÷ 4	8
7 × 4	48	42 ÷ 7	4
7 × 6	32	18 ÷ 2	6
6 × 3	42	24 ÷ 6	4

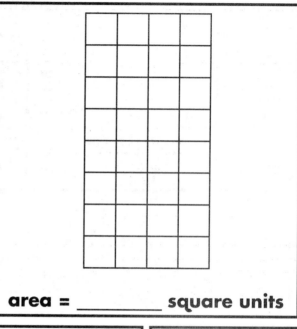

area = _____ square units

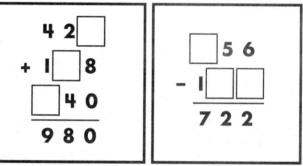

Reggie runs 3 miles a day, 2 times a week. How many miles will he have ran in 4 weeks?

502, 527, _____, _____, _____

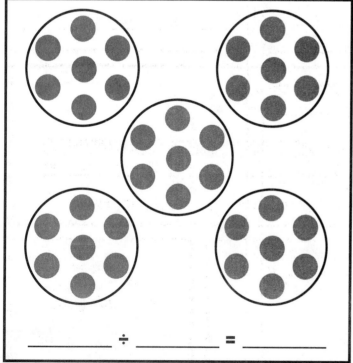

_____ ÷ _____ = _____

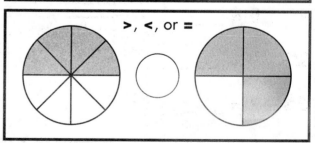

>, <, or =

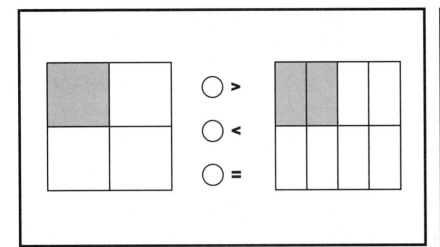

○ >

○ <

○ =

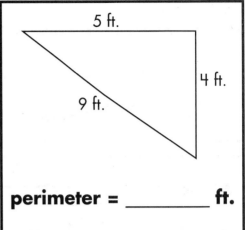

perimeter = _____ ft.

Landon went to his friend's party at 6:15 pm. He stayed for 3 hours and 25 minutes. What time did he leave the party?

$7 \times 4 =$ _____ $\times 7$

Bowling games cost $6 per game. How many games could Lindsey play if she had $30 to spend?

_____ ÷ _____ = _____

_____ × _____ = _____

$15 \div 3 =$ _____

$42 \div 6 =$ _____

$32 \div 4 =$ _____

$18 \div 6 =$ _____

$20 \div 4 =$ _____

$56 \div 7 =$ _____

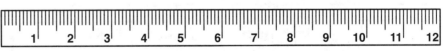

to the nearest quarter inch = _____ inches

April sold 8 raffle tickets at $5 each. How much money did she collect?

8 groups

6 in each group

_____ in all

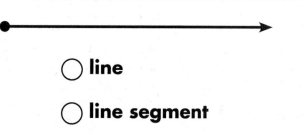

○ line

○ line segment

○ ray

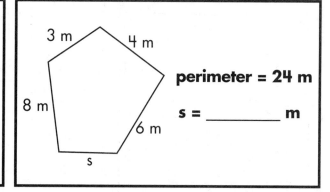

perimeter = 24 m

s = _____ m

$3 \times 4 \times 6 = (3 \times 4) \times 6$

true   **false**

Label each fraction on the number line. Compare.

0 |————|————|————|————|————|————| 1

$\dfrac{3}{6}$ ◯ $\dfrac{4}{6}$

Corbin brought 2 cases of water to his family reunion. Each case contained 24 bottles of water. At the end of the day, only 5 bottles of water were left. How many bottles did the family drink?

_____ **bottles**

$24 \div \underline{\quad} = 6$

---

7 rows

_____ in each row

42 in all

---

6 × 4 =	
7 × 5 =	
6 × 7 =	
7 × 3 =	
8 × 4 =	
6 × 8 =	
0 × 4 =	
1 × 7 =	

```
  428
  152
+ 137
```

Kristoff has 48 mL of liquid in a beaker. He added some more liquid. Then, he had 73 mL. How many mL of liquid did he add?

Draw perpendicular lines.

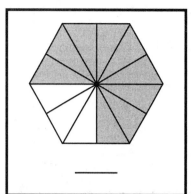

_____

$3 \times 20 =$ _____

$(3 \times 10) + (3 \times$ ___ $)$

6 × 7	
9 × 6	
5 × 8	
9 × 5	
7 × 7	
8 × 6	
6 × 6	
7 × 8	

Roberto went to a football game. The game started at 7:05 pm and lasted 2 hours and 38 minutes. What time did the game end?

about ____ inches long

82 counters

Take 10 away

8 rows of _____

$64 \div$ _____ $= 8$

Write a story to solve $28 \div 7$.

$$\begin{array}{r} 395 \\ + \ 358 \\ \hline \end{array}$$

_____

_____

_____

_____

_____

$$\frac{2}{8} \bigcirc \frac{7}{8}$$

$\bigcirc$ > $\bigcirc$ < $\bigcirc$ =

× 8	
4	
7	
8	
6	
0	
10	

÷ 6	
24	
36	
6	
18	
42	
48	

Yuri bought new sneakers online. He bought two pairs, each for $20. He had a coupon for $5 off the total purchase, and paid $6 for shipping. How much did he spend in all? Show your work

81 in all

_____ rows

9 in each row

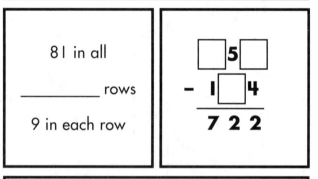

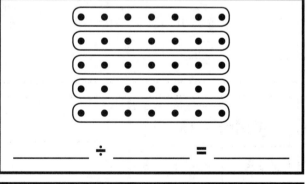

_____ ÷ _____ = _____

316, 301, _____, _____, _____

A fence is shaped like a rectangle. One side measures 6 feet and another side measures 8 feet. What is the area of the fenced-in space?

area = _____ × _____ = _____

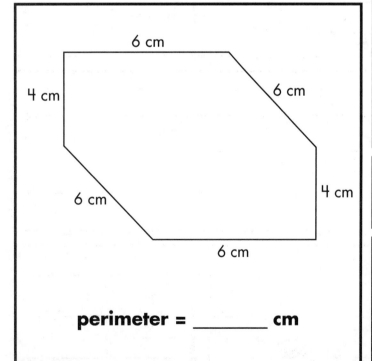

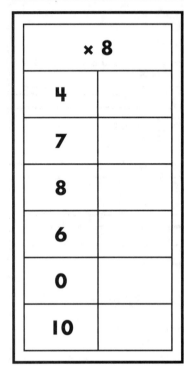

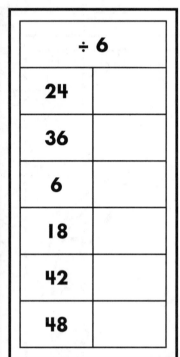

6 cm

4 cm

6 cm

6 cm

4 cm

6 cm

perimeter = _____ cm

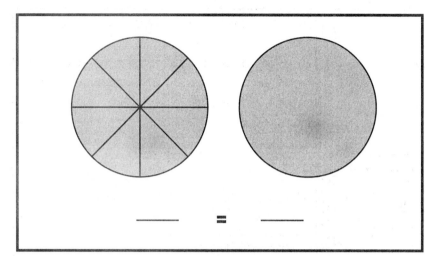

——— **=** ———

Trace the parallel sides in red.

What time is it? _____

What time was it 65 minutes ago? _____

What time will it be in 65 minutes? _____

204 + 387 is about _____ hundreds.

Bryce eats 2 servings of fruit each day. How many servings of fruit does he eat in one week?

Rule: ÷ 3	
15	
	4
6	
	1
24	
	3

0 _____ 1

☐   ☐

quadrilateral

_____ **sides**

_____ **angles**

$\dfrac{4}{5}$ ◯ $\dfrac{1}{3}$

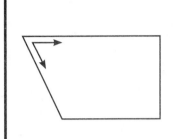
- ○ **right angle**
- ○ **obtuse angle**
- ○ **acute angle**

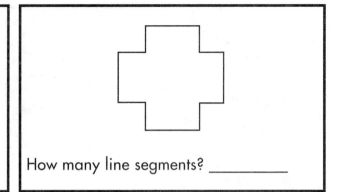

How many line segments? _____

7 groups

6 counters in each group

_____ counters in all

Draw a picture to solve 40 ÷ 5 = _____.

Start time: 10:30 am

Elapsed time: 5 hours 40 minutes

End time: _____ : _____

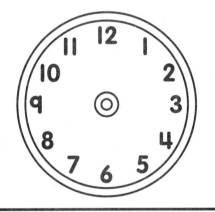

36 ÷ _____ = 4

403
− 248

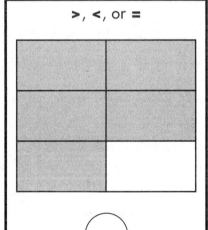

>, <, or =

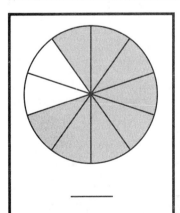

_____

9 ft.

8 ft.

area = _____ sq. ft.

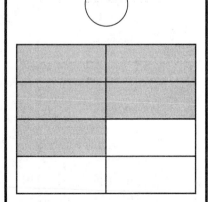

Name _____

$\dfrac{1}{2}$ ◯ $\dfrac{1}{3}$

◯ >   ◯ <   ◯ =

Start time: 7:54 am

End time: 10:05 pm

Elapsed time: _____

hours _____ minutes

If $7 \times 8 =$ _____,

then _____ $\div 8 = 7$.

Dimitri's fish tank holds 28 liters of water. He uses a bucket that holds 4 liters of water to empty the tank. How many times will he have to fill the bucket to empty the tank?

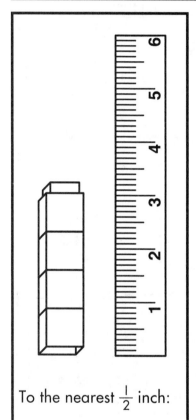

To the nearest $\dfrac{1}{2}$ inch:

_____ **inches**

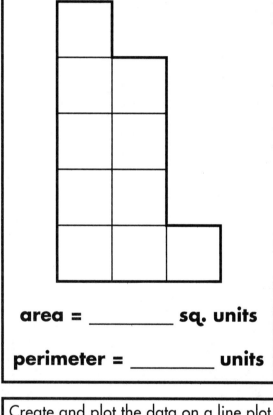

area = _____ **sq. units**

perimeter = _____ **units**

Gigi is pet-sitting some dogs. If she has 8 bones, and she gives each dog 2 bones, how many dogs is she pet sitting?

$14 \div$ _____ $= 7$

4 groups

_____ in each

28 in all

Create and plot the data on a line plot. Don't forget a title!

$\dfrac{1}{2}, \dfrac{3}{4}, \dfrac{1}{2}, \dfrac{3}{4}, \dfrac{1}{4}, \dfrac{3}{4}, \dfrac{1}{2}, 1, 1, \dfrac{1}{2}, \dfrac{1}{4}, \dfrac{1}{2}$

_____

⟵————————————————————⟶

>, <, or =

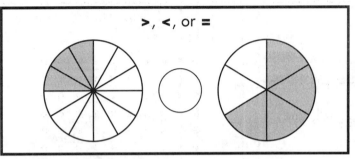

÷ 4	
	3
	6
	7
	2
	1
	5

× 3	
6	
5	
4	
8	
0	
9	

Circle to show 7 rows of 6. Complete the division fact.

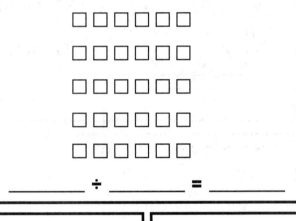

_____ ÷ _____ = _____

425
+ [ ]
789

727
- [ ]
513

Miguel baked cookies with his mom for the bake sale. They made 4 batches of chocolate chip and 2 batches of raisin oatmeal. Each batch had 8 cookies. How many cookies did they make in all?

3 cm   3 cm

4 cm

4 cm

4 cm

10 cm

perimeter = _____ cm

9, _____, 27, 36, _____, _____

2 × 48

(2 × 40) + (2 × _____)

(_____) + (_____) = _____

○ **22 minutes past 6**

○ **22 minutes to 6**

○ **22 minutes to 7**

Draw a rhombus. Divide it into 4 equal parts.

Draw 4 different quadrilaterals.

352 + 412 = _____

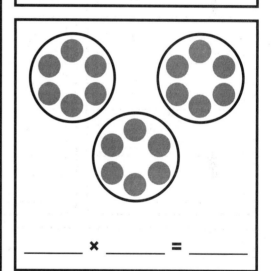

_____ × _____ = _____

Rule: add 6	
2	
4	
6	
8	
10	

Complete the number line to show that $\frac{1}{2}$ and $\frac{4}{8}$ are equal.

0                 $\frac{1}{2}$ 1

Rounded to nearest ten is about:

$$\begin{array}{r} 512 \\ -\ 378 \\ \hline \end{array}$$

$$\begin{array}{r} \\ -\ \\ \hline \end{array}$$

7 × 18 =
7 × (9 + 9) =
(7 × 9) + (7 × 9)

true   **false**

Divide each rectangle to show $\frac{4}{8} = \frac{2}{4}$.

6 × 16

(6 × _____) + (6 × 6)

_____ + _____ = _____

Start time: 9:04 am

Elapsed time: 3 hours 16 minutes

End time: _____:_____ **am/pm**

Write a story to solve 8 × 5 = _____.

_____

_____

_____

_____

6 in.

8 in.

area = _____ sq. in.

perimeter = _____ in.

(6 × 7) × 2 = _____ × (7 × 2)

9 groups

8 in each group

_____ in all

2	**× 8**	**16**
4		**12**
3		**15**
6		**24**
5		**20**
7		**28**
9		**27**
8		**24**

45
445
+ 44

Trace the perpendicular lines in red.

Yolanda leaves for gymnastics at 3:45 pm. She gets home at 6:05 pm. How long was she gone for?

_____ **hours** _____ **minutes**

64 in all

_____ equal groups

8 in each group

Five groups, 6 in each group = _____ in all.

Angelo had 4 friends over. Each friend drank 2 glasses of lemonade. Angelo´s brother had 1 glass of lemonade. How many glasses of lemonade did they drink in all?

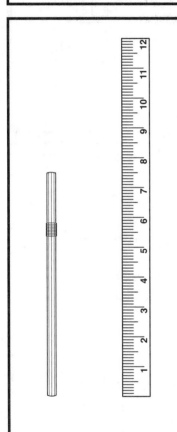

_____ **inches long**

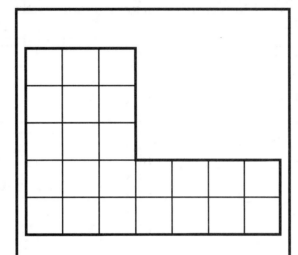

area = _____ **square units**

perimeter = _____ **units**

Color to show $\frac{4}{10}$.

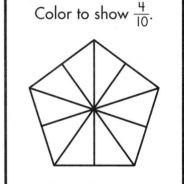

27 ÷ 3 =

red	
white	
yellow	
pink	

Key: = 4 flowers

Which color flower does the garden have the most of? _____
Which color flower does the garden have the least of? _____
How many flowers in the garden are red? _____
How many more yellow than pink flowers are in the garden?

_____

Five students shared 45 counters equally.

_____ **counters each.**

485 – 214 is about ○ **480 – 215.**

  ○ **490 – 210.**

  ○ **480 – 200.**

12 ÷ 3	
15 ÷ 3	
24 ÷ 3	
30 ÷ 3	
27 ÷ 3	
3 ÷ 3	
9 ÷ 3	

6 × 1	
8 × 4	
4 × 4	
3 × 4	
6 × 3	
4 × 6	
6 × 6	

_____ ÷ _____ = _____

a cup of tea	a popsicle stick
less than 1 L	**less than 1 g**
about 1 L	**about 1 g**
more than 1 L	**more than 1 g**

Draw a picture to solve 35 ÷ 5 = _____.

>, <, or =

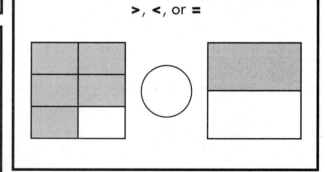

515, 500, _____, _____, _____

Javier has 3 folders saved on his tablet. Each folder has 6 games in it. How many games does he have in all?

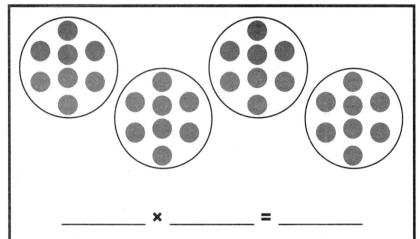

_____ × _____ = _____

4 × 14

(4 × 7) + (4 × _____)

28 + _____ = _____

Color the even products blue and the odd answers yellow.

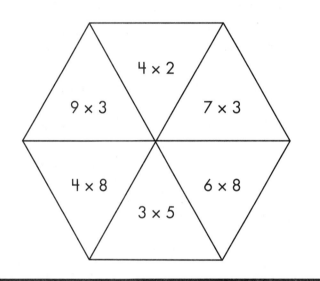

If 4 × ☐ = 28,
then 28 ÷ ☐ = 4.

Everett has $18. He is saving money to buy a $40 scooter. He earns $4 in allowance and $6 for babysitting. How much more money does he need to buy the scooter?

÷ 6	
54	
48	
42	
30	
36	

Split the number line into sixths. Label each part.

|←———————————————————————————————→|

Kaylee has twin baby brothers. Each baby wears 3 outfits a day. How many outfits do the babies wear each day?

100 in all

10 rows

_____ in each row

○ **trapezoid**

○ **quadrilateral**

○ **pentagon**

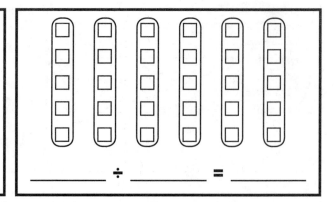

_____ ÷ _____ = _____

8 × 12

(8 × 6) + (8 × _____)

_____ + _____ = _____

>, <, or =

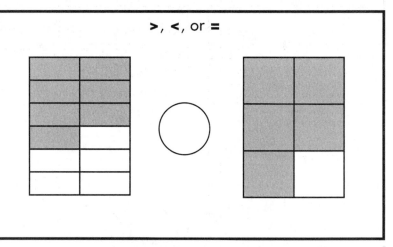

○

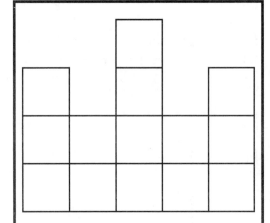

area = _____ square units

perimeter = _____ units

6 × 9 = 9 × ▢

56 in all

7 equal groups

_____ in each group

Follow the path of the even quotients.

START	
36 ÷ 9	35 ÷ 7
12 ÷ 3	16 ÷ 2
40 ÷ 8	16 ÷ 4
24 ÷ 6	20 ÷ 5
42 ÷ 7	20 ÷ 4
28 ÷ 7	42 ÷ 6
8 ÷ 4	56 ÷ 8
FINISH	

```
  344
  112
+ 178
```

8 in.

6 in.

area = _____ square inches

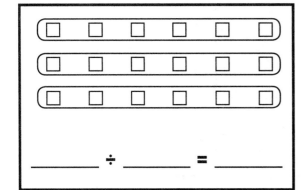

_____ ÷ _____ = _____

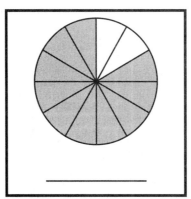

_____

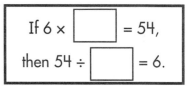

If 6 × ⬚ = 54,

then 54 ÷ ⬚ = 6.

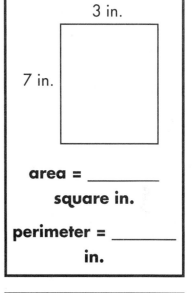

3 in.

7 in.

area = _____ **square in.**

perimeter = _____ **in.**

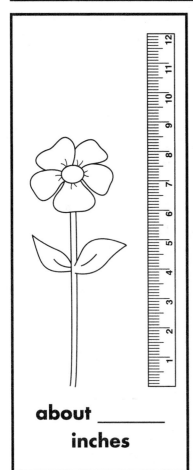

about _____
inches

Kaden's swim practice started at 4:30 pm. Practice lasted 1 hour and 15 minutes. After practice, he went out for dinner for 50 minutes. What time did he get home?

Four students share 5 packs of markers. Each pack of markers has 8 markers in it. How many markers does each student get?

72 ÷ _____ = 9

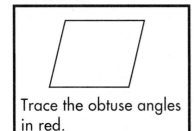

Trace the obtuse angles in red.

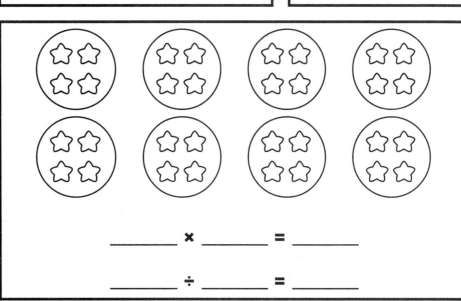

_____ × _____ = _____

_____ ÷ _____ = _____

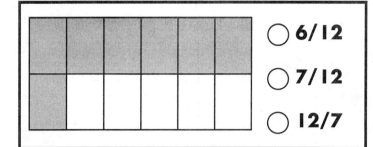

○ **6/12**

○ **7/12**

○ **12/7**

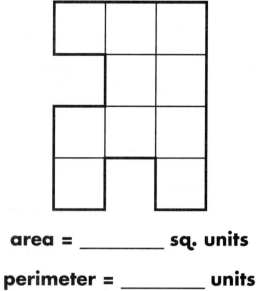

area = _____ sq. units

perimeter = _____ units

3 × 7	
4 × 8	
6 × 7	
5 × 8	
6 × 9	
8 × 3	
6 × 5	

48 ÷ 8	
32 ÷ 4	
16 ÷ 2	
30 ÷ 5	
36 ÷ 4	
81 ÷ 9	
42 ÷ 6	

$$507 - 489$$

$$507 + 489$$

Oscar had 35 strawberries. He ate 5. He shared the rest of them among 5 friends. How many strawberries does each friend get?

Draw a picture to solve 56 ÷ 7.

(4 × 8) × 2 = _____ × (_____ × 2)

>, <, or =

$\dfrac{4}{6}$ ○ $\dfrac{3}{6}$

> , < , or =

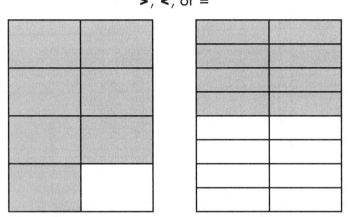

A square has a perimeter of 36 cm. What is the length of each side?

Devon had 32 trading cards. He divided the cards evenly among himself and his 3 friends. Draw a picture and write an equation to match.

828 is about _____ hundreds.

Draw a quadrilateral with four equal sides but no right angles.

Rule: × 6	
6	
2	
7	
8	
9	
0	

Split the number line into fifths. Label each fraction.

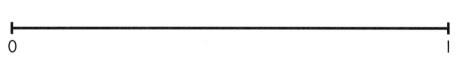

0   1

12 × 2 = (6 ×2) + (6 × 2)

_____ + _____ = 24

12 × 2 = _____

45 in all

5 groups

_____ in each group

63 counters divided into 7 groups

○ **7 × 63**

○ **63 – 7**

○ **63 ÷ 7**

Complete to solve 24 ÷ 3.

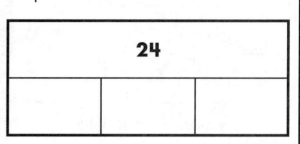

There were 3 flags. Each flag had 6 stars on it. How many stars were on the flags in all?

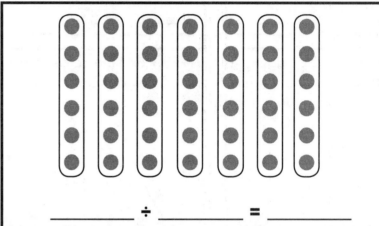

_____ ÷ _____ = _____

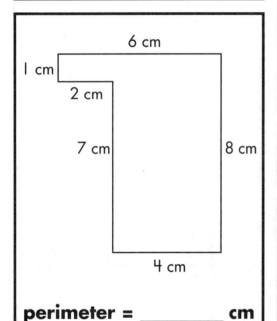

6 cm

1 cm

2 cm

7 cm

8 cm

4 cm

perimeter = _____ cm

15 ÷ _____ = 3

4 rows

8 in each row

_____ in all

6	×3	18
2		14
3		12
5		15
4		20
6		24
4		28

Kimmi has 40 mL of water. She divides the water equally into 4 separate beakers. How many mL does each beaker hold?

>, <, or =

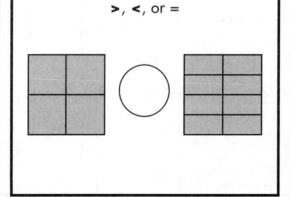

A jug of milk holds

◯ **about 1 liter.**

◯ **less than 1 liter.**

◯ **more than 1 liter.**

Dante has $35. He spends $10 on a ticket to the fair. He buys 2 drinks for $2 each and a bag of popcorn for $3. How much money is left?

(8 × _____) = (7 × _____)

Mr. Franco is putting a fence around his garden. Two sides of the garden are 8 feet, and the other two sides are 7 feet. How many feet of fencing will Mr. Franco need?

---

8)$\overline{64}$ = _____

7)$\overline{42}$ = _____

8)$\overline{32}$ = _____

7)$\overline{56}$ = _____

10)$\overline{80}$ = _____

2)$\overline{16}$ = _____

9)$\overline{18}$ = _____

4)$\overline{20}$ = _____

6)$\overline{24}$ = _____

Start time: 8:07 am

Elapsed time: 5 hours 28 minutes

End time: _____:_____ **am/pm**

Divide the square into 6 equal parts. Label.

---

530 + 203 = _____

---

7)$\overline{63}$

The dividend is _____ .

The divisor is _____ .

The quotient is _____ .

Write a story to solve 32 ÷ 8.

_____

_____

_____

_____

_____

A pizza is cut into 8 slices. Luke eats 2 slices. How much of the pizza did he eat?

12 ÷ 3	
16 ÷ 4	
24 ÷ 6	
28 ÷ 4	
21 ÷ 3	
36 ÷ 9	
42 ÷ 6	

6 × 7	
	4 × 6
5 × 5	
	8 × 4
3 × 8	
	8 × 7
6 × 6	

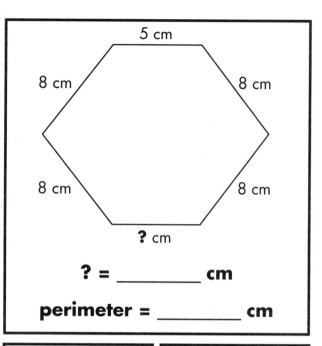

? = _____ cm

perimeter = _____ cm

>, <, or =

$\dfrac{8}{8}$ ◯ $\dfrac{2}{3}$

$\dfrac{8}{2}$ = _____

Erik had 4 bags of popcorn. Each bag contained 20 pieces of popcorn. He ate 1 bag and gave 1 bag to his sister. How many pieces of popcorn were left?

63, _____, _____, 36, _____, 18, 9, 0

_____   ◯   _____

6 cm

4 cm

area = _____ square cm

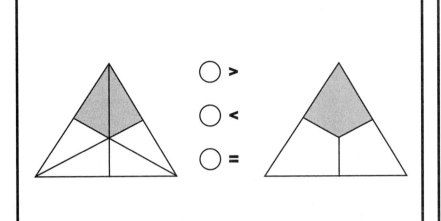

○ >
○ <
○ =

There are 63 seats in a movie theater. There are 9 rows. How many seats in each row?

_____ ÷ _____ = _____

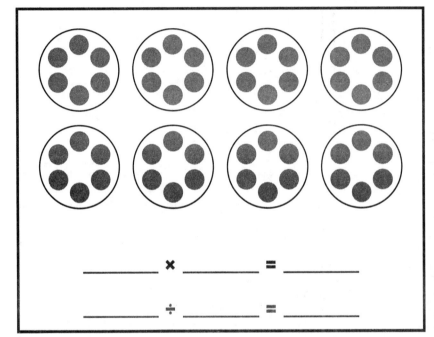

214 is about _____ hundreds.

Color to show $\frac{1}{5}$.

_____ × _____ = _____

_____ ÷ _____ = _____

	÷ 3
15	
	6
27	
	4
30	

Draw a number line divided into sevenths. Label each seventh.

Shamar had some counters. She divided them evenly into 6 groups. There were 6 counters in each group. How many counters did she have in all?

487
− 235

○ **2/5**
○ **3/5**
○ **4/5**

Trace the right angles in red.

5 × 13

(5 × 10) + (5 × _____)

_____ + _____ = _____

Split into two rectangles.
Find the area of each
rectangle. Add.

2 m

8 m   6 m

2 m

2 × 8 = _____ , 6 × 2 = _____

_____ + _____ = _____

area of total shape = _____ sq. meters

>, <, or =

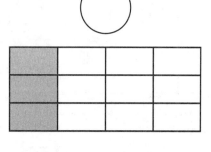

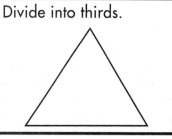

72 ÷ _____ = 9

Divide into thirds.

Jaya builds 6 towers.
Each tower uses
8 blocks. How many
blocks did she use
in all?

Start time: 6:35 pm

Elapse time: 3 hours and 22 minutes

End time: _____ ; _____**am/pm**

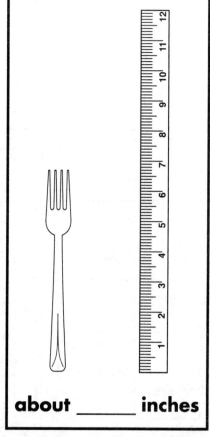

about _____ inches

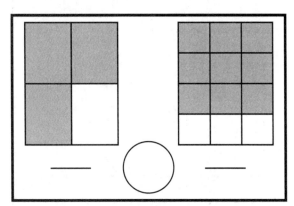

____ ◯ ____

Mya ate $\frac{3}{8}$ of a pizza. Alberto ate $\frac{1}{4}$ of a pizza. Who ate more?

$6 \times 12 =$
$(6 \times 3) + (6 \times 3)$
true   **false**

Diego's family spent the day at the beach. They left their house at 8:45 am and got home at 3:30 pm. How long were they gone?

Write a story to solve $7 \times 8 =$ _____.

_____

_____

_____

_____

_____

_____

_____

_____

_____ ÷ _____ =

_____

Divide and label 4 equal parts.

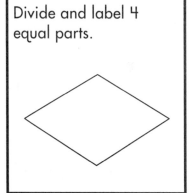

900 – 874 = _____

Draw a picture and write an equation to solve 4 equal groups of 9.

Luis had 42 mL of water. He added more. Then, he had 70 mL. How much water did he add?

Label $\frac{3}{8}$ and $\frac{8}{8}$.

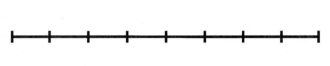

3 × 6 =	
6 × 4 =	
4 × 7 =	
6 × 5 =	
6 × 8 =	
9 × 4 =	
9 × 3 =	

27 ÷ 3 =	
32 ÷ 4 =	
16 ÷ 4 =	
25 ÷ 5 =	
40 ÷ 8 =	
36 ÷ 6 =	
18 ÷ 3 =	

What time is it? _____

What time was it 3 hours and 15 minutes ago? _____

$$\frac{1}{4} = \frac{\square}{8}$$

$$\frac{15}{3} = \underline{\qquad}$$

Izzy made 2 salads for her and her sister. Each salad used 4 baby carrots, 2 pieces of celery, and 5 slices of cucumbers. How many vegetables were used in all?

Give the graph a title and label both the x- and y-axis. Write a question to match the graph.

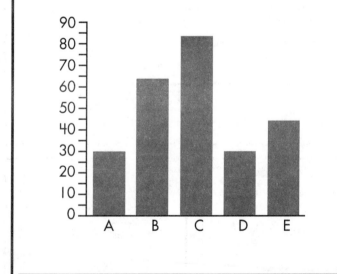

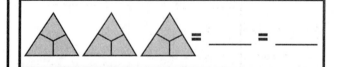 = _____ = _____

Brooklyn's favorite TV show comes on at 8:00 pm. It is 6:15 pm now. How much longer does Brooklyn have to wait until her show starts?

886 − 132 is about

○ **700**

○ **760**

○ **800**

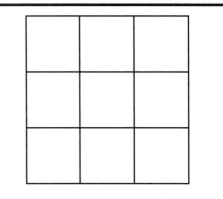

How many squares in all? _____

3 ft.

7 ft.

7 ft.

10 ft.

3 ft.

10 ft.

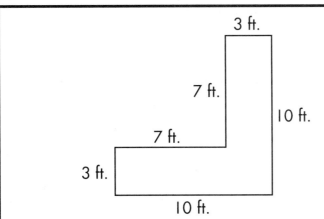

Split to find the area of the two rectangles. Add.

_____ + _____ = _____

area of total shape = _____ sq. units

780 − 598 = _____

Holly made 4 mugs of hot chocolate at her sleepover. She had 24 mini marshmallows, and put an even number into each mug. How many mini marshmallows did each girl get?

Rule: ÷4	
28	
	6
12	
	5
32	

Start time: 8:30 am
Elapsed time: 2 hours, 25 minutes
End time: _____ : _____ **am/pm**

8:30 am

Avery has a dollhouse. There are 5 rooms in the house, and each room in the house has 4 pieces of furniture. Two of the pieces of furniture break. How many does she have left?

$$\frac{1}{4} = \frac{\square}{8}$$

A part of a line that includes two endpoints and all the points in between is called a

○ **line.**

○ **ray.**

○ **line segment.**

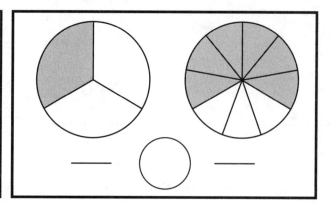

____ ◯ ____

---

7 × 24

(7 × 20) + (_____ × _____)

_____ + _____ = _____

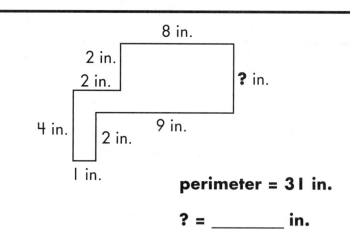

perimeter = 31 in.

? = _____ in.

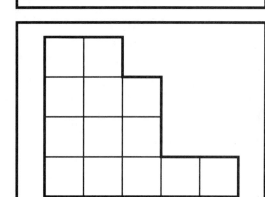

each square = 1 cm

area = _____ sq. cm

perimeter = _____ cm

---

100 ÷ _____ = 10

$\frac{3}{5}$ ◯ $\frac{1}{10}$

Follow the path of the odd quotients.

START	
63 ÷ 7	30 ÷ 5
42 ÷ 6	28 ÷ 4
12 ÷ 3	21 ÷ 7
32 ÷ 8	15 ÷ 5
8 ÷ 8	20 ÷ 4
54 ÷ 6	36 ÷ 9
FINISH	

---

a bunch of bananas

more than 1 gram

less than 1 gram

Start time: 7:50 am

End time: 1:05 pm

Elapsed time:

_____ hours _____ minutes

---

(42) $\begin{array}{r}3\\ \times\,3\\\hline\end{array}$	(36) $\begin{array}{r}3\\ \times\,4\\\hline\end{array}$	(45) $\begin{array}{r}3\\ \times\,5\\\hline\end{array}$	(40) $\begin{array}{r}3\\ \times\,6\\\hline\end{array}$
(56) $\begin{array}{r}3\\ \times\,7\\\hline\end{array}$	(49) $\begin{array}{r}3\\ \times\,8\\\hline\end{array}$	(54) $\begin{array}{r}3\\ \times\,9\\\hline\end{array}$	(48) $\begin{array}{r}4\\ \times\,4\\\hline\end{array}$
(81) $\begin{array}{r}4\\ \times\,5\\\hline\end{array}$	(72) $\begin{array}{r}4\\ \times\,6\\\hline\end{array}$	(64) $\begin{array}{r}4\\ \times\,7\\\hline\end{array}$	(63) $\begin{array}{r}4\\ \times\,8\\\hline\end{array}$
(12) $\begin{array}{r}4\\ \times\,9\\\hline\end{array}$	(0) $\begin{array}{r}5\\ \times\,5\\\hline\end{array}$	(11) $\begin{array}{r}5\\ \times\,6\\\hline\end{array}$	(100) $\begin{array}{r}5\\ \times\,7\\\hline\end{array}$

(18) $\begin{array}{r} 5 \\ \times\,8 \\ \hline \end{array}$	(15) $\begin{array}{r} 5 \\ \times\,9 \\ \hline \end{array}$	(12) $\begin{array}{r} 6 \\ \times\,6 \\ \hline \end{array}$	(9) $\begin{array}{r} 6 \\ \times\,7 \\ \hline \end{array}$
(16) $\begin{array}{r} 6 \\ \times\,8 \\ \hline \end{array}$	(27) $\begin{array}{r} 6 \\ \times\,9 \\ \hline \end{array}$	(24) $\begin{array}{r} 7 \\ \times\,7 \\ \hline \end{array}$	(21) $\begin{array}{r} 7 \\ \times\,8 \\ \hline \end{array}$
(32) $\begin{array}{r} 7 \\ \times\,9 \\ \hline \end{array}$	(28) $\begin{array}{r} 8 \\ \times\,8 \\ \hline \end{array}$	(24) $\begin{array}{r} 8 \\ \times\,9 \\ \hline \end{array}$	(20) $\begin{array}{r} 9 \\ \times\,9 \\ \hline \end{array}$
(35) $\begin{array}{r} 10 \\ \times\,10 \\ \hline \end{array}$	(30) $\begin{array}{r} 11 \\ \times\,1 \\ \hline \end{array}$	(25) $\begin{array}{r} 12 \\ \times\,0 \\ \hline \end{array}$	(36) $\begin{array}{r} 12 \\ \times\,1 \\ \hline \end{array}$

(63) $\begin{array}{r} 2 \\ \times 3 \\ \hline \end{array}$	(72) $\begin{array}{r} 4 \\ \times 3 \\ \hline \end{array}$	(56) $\begin{array}{r} 5 \\ \times 3 \\ \hline \end{array}$	(48) $\begin{array}{r} 6 \\ \times 3 \\ \hline \end{array}$
(18) $\begin{array}{r} 7 \\ \times 3 \\ \hline \end{array}$	(18) $\begin{array}{r} 8 \\ \times 3 \\ \hline \end{array}$	(16) $\begin{array}{r} 9 \\ \times 3 \\ \hline \end{array}$	(14) $\begin{array}{r} 2 \\ \times 4 \\ \hline \end{array}$
(10) $\begin{array}{r} 5 \\ \times 4 \\ \hline \end{array}$	(12) $\begin{array}{r} 6 \\ \times 4 \\ \hline \end{array}$	(14) $\begin{array}{r} 7 \\ \times 4 \\ \hline \end{array}$	(16) $\begin{array}{r} 8 \\ \times 4 \\ \hline \end{array}$
(0) $\begin{array}{r} 9 \\ \times 4 \\ \hline \end{array}$	(2) $\begin{array}{r} 2 \\ \times 5 \\ \hline \end{array}$	(4) $\begin{array}{r} 6 \\ \times 5 \\ \hline \end{array}$	(6) $\begin{array}{r} 7 \\ \times 6 \\ \hline \end{array}$

⑱	⑮	⑫	⑥
8 $\times 6$	8 $\times 7$	9 $\times 8$	9 $\times 7$

⑧	㉗	㉔	㉑
2 $\times 7$	2 $\times 8$	2 $\times 9$	9 $\times 2$

㉜	㉘	㉔	⑳
8 $\times 2$	7 $\times 2$	6 $\times 2$	5 $\times 2$

㊷	㉚	⑩	㊱
3 $\times 2$	2 $\times 2$	2 $\times 1$	2 $\times 0$

Answer Key

Day 1

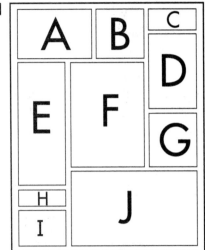

Day 2

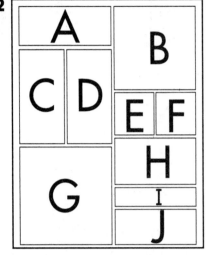

Day 3

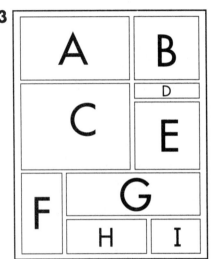

Day 4

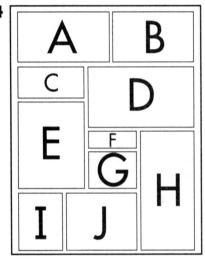

Week 1, Day 1 (page 17)

A. 3×5=15; B. 330, 300; C. 42; D. 4:10;
E. ounces, pounds; F. square; G. 8 teams;
H. 916; I. 8, 12, 16; J. 10, 4, 2

Week 1, Day 2 (page 18)

A. 6; B. 95; C. 40, 60, 80, 100, 120, 140;
D. Check students' work. E. 200 + 40 + 1; F.
227; G. clockwise from 15: 25, 10, 50, 30,
40, 5, 35, 20, 45; H. 16 square units;
I. 2 hours, 15 minutes; J. Plot points on
number line in the order of C, A, D, B,
rounded to 10, 20, 10, 20.

Week 1, Day 3 (page 19)

A. 8:20; B. Check students' work.

C. blue: 2 × 7, 6 × 4, red: 5 × 5, 3 ×5,
green: 2 × 3, 8 × 2; D. 934; E. <; F. 32;
G. 10; H. 4; I. 4 × 6 = 24

Week 1, Day 4 (page 20)

A. 10 pounds; B. $\frac{1}{2}$; C. 7,460, 7,500; D. Q,
Q, N, N; E. $33; F. 500; G. 3; H. 48;
I. 229; J. Aimee is 13, Trey is 7.

Week 2, Day 1 (page 21)

A. $22; B. 8 ÷ 2=4; C. 8; D. Clock should
show 3:48. E. 3 $\frac{1}{2}$ inches; F. 2 × 3 + 6 + 8,
2 × 5 + 3 + 7, etc. G. 7 tens 9 ones; H. 185;
I. Check students' work. J. Check students'
work.

Answer Key

Week 2, Day 2 (page 22)
A. 363; B. $\frac{4}{6}$, $\frac{2}{6}$; C. Clocks should read 7:25.
D. 18; E. 6; F. 154; G. Each should equal 24;
H. 8 sq. units; I. 633, 653, 673; J. 77

Week 2, Day 3 (page 23)
A. Yes, she read 106 minutes, which is greater than 100; B. 1 hour 30 minutes;
C. 14 in.; D. 7; E. Check students' work.
F. $3 \times 7 = 21$; G. 9; H. 980, 1,000; I. 850

Week 2, Day 4 (page 24)
A. less than 1 liter; B. $4 \times 3 = 12$; C. 9;
D. 12, 13, 16; E. 2, 4; F. 7; G. 280; H. 0, 7, 14, 21, 28, 35, 42, 49, 56, 63, 70;
I. scale; J. <

Week 3, Day 1 (page 25)
A. 12; B. 15; C. 787; D. Check students' work. E. 28, 16, 24, 36, 32, 20; F. Answers should describe 24 divided equally by 3.
G. 2; H. 64; I. 28, 28, 7; J. 62

Week 3, Day 2 (page 26)
A. ; B. 6, 5, 30; C. 30, 18, 48, 42, 36, 60; D. 7, 2, 6, 4, 8, 3, 5;
E. 45 minutes; F. $\frac{2}{3}$; G. clockwise from 9: 15, 6, 30, 18, 24, 3, 21, 12, 27; H. 9, 19, 28, 38, 40, 41; I. 512, 532, 542; J. $2\frac{1}{2}$ inches

Week 3, Day 3 (page 27)
A. 5:42; B. 8; C. 14, 3, 1; D. 430;
E. $800 - 100 = 700$, 700; F. 0, 9, 18, 27, 36, 45, 54, 63, 72, 81, 90; G. 24, 30, 36;
H. 18; I. 8, 56, 8

Week 3, Day 4 (page 28)
A. Check students' work. B. 15; C. 4; D. 1 hour 30 minutes; E. Sidney; F. 6; G. 6, 5; H. 12, 12, 21, 18, 20, 14, 24, 30; I. 63, 7, 7, 63; J. one pound

Week 4, Day 1 (page 29)
A. 47 ounces; B. 3, 6, 18; C. 825; D. Clock should show 7:18. E. 32, 64, 56, 72, 40, 48, 24; F. 4, 8, 32, 32; G. 375, 375, 653; H. 63; I. 174; J. 300, 400, 300, 400, 300

Week 4, Day 2 (page 30)
A. 14; B. clockwise from 12: 48, 24, 30, 36, 18, 60, 54, 42, 0; C. 24, 48, 60, 72, 84;
D. $12 \div 3 = 4$; E. 4; F. Check students' work.
G. blue: $16 \div 4$, purple: $36 \div 6$, green: 6×2, yellow: $20 \div 2$; H. 3, 30, 60, 90; I. 750, 800, 850; J. $4\frac{1}{2}$

Week 4, Day 3 (page 31)
A. <; B. 950, 1,000; C. 116 miles; D. 5;
E. 6; F. 10, 15, 20, 25, 30, 35, 40, 45, 50;
G. 6, 6, 6, 6, $30 \div 5 = 6$; H. 24; I. 415

Week 4, Day 4 (page 32)
A. 24 cm; B. $14 \div 2 = 7$ each; C. 1,000;
D. Circle all but the pentagon. E. trapezoid, 4; F. 9; G. 1; H. clock should show 7:10;
I. 239; J. >

Week 5, Day 1 (page 33)
A. one quarter, one dime, two nickels and one penny; B. =; C. 8; D. 8, 52; E. 0, 3, 6, 9, 12, 15, 18, 21, 24; F. Students should draw an octagon. G. 90; H. 270; I. 5; J. $5\frac{3}{4}$

Week 5, Day 2 (page 34)
A. 311; B. array with 4 rows of 7; C. 2, 4, 6, 8, 10, 5; D. Clocks should show 1:33. E. 8;
F. 6, 24, 24, 4; G. ; H. 2 hours 30 minutes; I. 116, 136, 146; J. true

Week 5, Day 3 (page 35)
A. $32 \div 4 = 8$; B. 7,490, 7,500, 4,090, 4,100; C. clockwise from 9: 21, 3, 6, 24, 18, 12, 27, 30, 15; D. 27, 9, 3; E. 21; F. 24, 12, 14, 28, 15, 18; G. Number line should be labeled $\frac{1}{3}$, $\frac{2}{3}$, $\frac{3}{3}$; H. 18 cm; I. 40, 80, 120

Answer Key

Week 5, Day 4 (page 36)
A. 1 mile; B. 8; C. 628; D. 4 goals; E. 8, 2, 2; F. 9; G. 6; H. 1, 2, 3, 4, 5, 6; I. 9:12; J. 24

Week 6, Day 1 (page 37)
A. $\frac{5}{6}$; B. 49; C. 890; D. 210; E. 0, 8, 16, 24, 32 40, 48, 56, 64, 72, 80; F. 4; G. 12; H. 7; I. 8; J. row 1: 4, 8, 4, row 2: 9, 14, 12, row 3: 20, 26, row 4: 45

Week 6, Day 2 (page 38)
A. <; B. 18, 6; C. 0, 7, 14, 21, 28, 35, 42, 49, 56, 63, 70; D. 5, 2, 6, 10, 8, 3, 7, 9, 1, 4; E. 350; F. 6; G. 10:10 am; H. 200 + 400 = 600; I. 9; J. 158

Week 6, Day 3 (page 39)
A. six hundreds, four ones; B. 5, 3 15; C. 4 × 2 = 8; D. 100; E. 6; F. 4, 6, 9, 3, 5, 8; G. 20, 5, 4; H. 8, 3; I. 108

Week 6, Day 4 (page 40)
A. 21; B. 2, 6, 12; C. 8; D. 2$\frac{3}{4}$; E. Clock should show 4:37. F. 998; G. 9; H. 15, 24, 18, 9, 12, 6, 21, 27, 3, 30; I. 25; J. 2

Week 7, Day 1 (page 41)
A. 32; B. 3; C. 9; D. 25, 30, 35; E. 10, 9, 8, 7, 6, 5, 4, 3, 2, 1; F. 4 × 6, 3 × 8, 6 × 4; G. Check students' work.; H. 645; I. about 10; J. $14, $21

Week 7, Day 2 (page 42)
A. 366; B. 100; C. 18; D. 8, 3, 10, 7, 9, 2, 1, 4, 5, 6; E. 120, 200, 300; F. 152; G. 1 hour 46 minutes; H. 383; I. 4; J. $\frac{4}{5}$

Week 7, Day 3 (page 43)
A. 6; B. 7:24; C. color 2 out of 6 ants, 1 out of 4 ants, 6 out of 12 ants; D. 9; E. 3, 6, 9, 12; F. 4 × 8, 4 × 4, 4 × 3, 4 × 6, 4 × 7, 4 × 5; G. =; H. 3; I. false

Week 7, Day 4 (page 44)
A. 4:25; B. 4 × 8 = 32; C. 9; D. 20; E. a. 3, 3, b. 2, 3, c. 2, 1, d. 5, 4; F. 6; G. 9; H. 5 $\frac{1}{2}$; I. 887; J. Check students' work.

Week 8, Day 1 (page 45)
A. 36; B. 250; C. 2,500; D. $\frac{4}{10}$; E. by row, left to right: 4, 16, 4, 16, 2, 2, 7, 5, 7, 5, 4, 4; F. 7 × 5 = 35; G. 6; H. 2; I. 970; J. Check students' work.

Week 8, Day 2 (page 46)
A. $7; B. row 1: 4, 6, 8, 10, 12, row 2: 6, 9, 12, 15, 18, row 3: 8, 12, 16, 20, 24, row 4: 10, 15, 20, 25, 30, row 5: 12, 18, 24, 30, 36; C. 6, 3, 2, 10, 8, 4, 5, 7, 9; D. 12:41; E. 740; F. 1997; G. 10; H. >; I. 110, 410, 510; J. 3, 6, 18

Week 8, Day 3 (page 47)
A. 15 ÷ 3; B. Check students' work.; C. red: 4 × 3, 4 × 6, 3 × 8, 6 × 5, blue: 5 × 3, 3 × 9, 9 × 9, 5 × 5; D. 8; E. 64; F. 8, 7, 6, 5, 4, 3, 2, 1; G. 7:10; H. square; I. gram

Week 8, Day 4 (page 48)
A. 2 hundreds + 4 tens + 8 ones; B. 12:45 pm; C. 81; D. 7 $\frac{1}{2}$; E. 3, 2, 9; F. 3; G. 180; H. Yes. Check students' work. I. 148; J. 15 ÷ 3, 9 ÷ 3, 6 ÷ 2

Week 9, Day 1 (page 49)
A. 28, 4, 7; B. 185; C. 331; D. 20; E. 14, 42, 63, 49, 56, 35, 7, 28, 21, 0, 70; F. 4:30, 5:00, 6:00, 7:00; G. 6; H. 873; I. 660, 700; J. >

Week 9, Day 2 (page 50)
A. 9; B. clockwise from 12: 30, 36, 18, 48, 42, 54, 24, 60, 0; C. 18, 20, 24, 28, 48, 42, 36, 30; D. 10 songs; E. 2, 4; F. 6, 7; G. 24, Check students' work. H. 6; I. 100; J. 16, 20, 24

Answer Key

Week 9, Day 3 (page 51)
A. more than 1 liter; B. 15, 2, 45, 3; C. top: 8, 7, 6, bottom: 6, 7, 8; D. 48; E. 24; F. 0, 10, 20, 30, 40, 50, 60, 70, 80, 90, 100; G. $\frac{2}{4}$, $\frac{3}{4}$, 1 or $\frac{4}{4}$; H. 5; I. pentagon

Week 9, Day 4 (page 52)
A. 6, 6, 6, 24 ÷ 4 = 6; B. 7; C. 2,170, 2,200; D. 9:50, 10:20, 10:40, 11:20; E. 21; F. 7; G. Check students' work. H. 8, 5, 9, 6, 7; I. 24; J. 4

Week 10, Day 1 (page 53)
A. 3, 7, 21; B. 50; C. 8; D. $6; E. 3, 3, 2, 6, 5, 4, 5, 6; F. red: 5 × 7, 7 × 7, 9 × 9, 3 × 7, blue: 6 × 8, 6 × 5, 4 × 7, 7 × 6; G. 60; H. 5; I. 141; J. Check students' work.

Week 10, Day 2 (page 54)
A. 643, 663, 703; B. 4 × 6, 8 × 3, 6 × 4; C. 4, 4, 7, 3, 6, 9, 3; D. 21, 24, 24, 27, 21, 24, 27; E. 30, 60, 90; F. 143; G. Check students' work. H. $\frac{7}{12}$; I. 837; J. $12

Week 10, Day 3 (page 55)
A. 8; B. Check students' work. C. trapezoid; D. 9; E. 7; F. 9, 8, 6, 6, 7; G. 12:15, 1:15, 2 hours 10 minutes; H. $\frac{4}{2}$; I. 994

Week 10, Day 4 (page 56)
A. 500 – 200; B. 16; C. 780, 800; D. June, 5, 2; E. 18, 15, 12, 9, 6; F. 7; G. 201; H. 5; I. $\frac{4}{8}$; J. 6, 3, 18, 6

Week 11, Day 1 (page 57)
A. 4 × 8 = 32; B. Check students' work. C. 70; D. 24; E. from top, left to right: 8, 16, 8, 16, 4, 4, 6, 6, 6, 6, 8, 16, 8; F. 5:20 pm; G. 747; H. 177; I. 24, 240, 24, 240; J. 32 ÷ 4

Week 11, Day 2 (page 58)
A. 3; B. 1, 20; C. 21, 30, 28, 15, 18, 24, 56, 32, 27, 36; D. 8, 4, 5, 10, 2, 6, 7, 9, 1; E. 5 liters; F. 1 gram; G. 6; H. $\frac{5}{8}$; I. 632; J. 6, 30, 5, 6

Week 11, Day 3 (page 59)
A. 42, 18; B. $8; C. from top, left to right: 12, 14, 16, 18, 20, 18, 21, 24, 27, 30, 24, 28, 32, 36, 40, 30, 35, 40, 45, 50, 36, 42, 48, 54, 60; D. 148; E. 27; F. 9, 8, 7, 6, 5, 4, 3, 2, 1; G. from left to right: $\frac{2}{8}$, $\frac{4}{8}$, $\frac{6}{8}$; H. 50 + 60 = 110; I. false

Week 11, Day 4 (page 60)
A. 600 + 400; B. 18, 3, 6; C. 40; D. Check students' work. E. 12:30 pm; F. 8; G. 176; H. 24, 16, 28, 36, 40, 12, 32, 8, 0, 20; I. Check students' work. J. Check students' work.

Week 12, Day 1 (page 61)
A. 4 × 3 = 12; B. 80, 160, 240, 320; C. 6; D. 8, 7, 6, 5, 4, 3, 2, 1; E. 6 $\frac{1}{2}$; F. 12, 18, 12, 24, 15, 16; G. 428; H. 7; I. 42, 6, 6, 6; J. 1 hour 35 minutes

Week 12, Day 2 (page 62)
A. 18; B. 2:27; C. 8, 7, 8, 7, 9, 4; D. 5, Check students' work. E. 78; F. 753; G. 24, Check students' work. H. 21; I. 80; J. $24

Week 12, Day 3 (page 63)
A. 20; B. 2; C. clockwise from 14: 35, 49, 7, 28, 56, 0, 63, 42, 70; D. 490, 550, 570; E. 42; F. 8, 9, 7, 4, 7, 1; G. Check students' work. H. Circle the first pair of lines I. =

Week 12, Day 4 (page 64)
A. 730 + 270; B. 4; C. true; D. 4:22, 4:42, 4:02; E. 4; F. 7; G. 610, 600; H. 1, 2, 1, 3, 1, 4, 1, 5, 1; I. 6, 2; J. 22

Week 13, Day 1 (page 65)
A. Check students' work. B. 9; C. 9;

Answer Key

D. 7 x 3=21; E. 0, 1, 4, 9, 16, 25, 36, 49, 64, 81, 100; F. 9 pieces; G. 8, 16, 40, 80; H. 1,254; I. 1 gram; J. 28

Week 13, Day 2 (page 66)

A. 16, 4, 4; B. 36; C. 1, 6, 4, 2, 8, 3, 9, 10, 5; D. 12, 10, 30, 18, 21, 42; E. 30, 60, 90; F. 316; G. from top to bottom, left to right: 55, 23, 32, 8, 17, 15, 1, 9, 6; H. 508; I. 742, 682; J. 24, Check students' work.

Week 13, Day 3 (page 67)

A. 5, 5; B. 10,000 liters; C. 18; D. 8; E. 6, 12, 18, 10, 20, 30, 14, 28, 42; F. 6, 12, 15, 18; G. The number line should be labeled $\frac{1}{4}$, $\frac{2}{4}$, $\frac{3}{4}$ with Point A at $\frac{3}{4}$. H. 15; I. $\frac{4}{6}$

Week 13, Day 4 (page 68)

A. 650 – 360; B. 3 hours 25 minutes; C. 81; D. blue: 3 crayons, yellow: 2 crayons, red: 4 crayons; E. green: 7 x 6, 5 x 8, 4 x 8, 6 x 6, 4 x 5, 6 x 8 yellow: 3 x 5, 5 x 5, 9 x 3, 7 x 7, 3 x 7, 9 x 7; F. 8; G. about 2 inches; H. 4, 9, 9, 3, 6, 8, 7, 7, 5; I. 955; J. 4, 4, quadrilateral or trapezoid

Week 14, Day 1 (page 69)

A. 63, 9, 7; B. 30; C. false; D. 6, 7, 8, 9; E. 30; F. 4:40; G. 965; H. 8; I. 3; J. 32, 4, 8

Week 14, Day 2 (page 70)

A. 20; B. 24; C. 12, 18, 6, 28, 45, 56; D. 2, 6, 8, 1, 5, 7, 9; E. 111; F. 981; G. 2 x 6 = 12, 2 x 4 = 8, 5 x 2 = 10, 2 x 3 = 6, 6 x 1 = 6, 2 x 3 = 6; H. 14; I. 8, 16; J. 730, 700

Week 14, Day 3 (page 71)

A. Jim= 60 inches, Sarah=58 inches; B. more than one liter; C. 6, Check students' work. D. 67; E. 21; F. 8, 16, 24, 32, 40; G. 5:45, Check students' work. H. 6, 6, 6; I. 240, 60, 240, 60

Week 14, Day 4 (page 72)

A. trapezoid or rhombus; B. 4, 9, 36; C. 4, 6; D. $\frac{3}{4} > \frac{4}{8}$; E. 4:55 pm; F. 3; G. 89; H. 4, 8, 5, 7, 10, 9, 2, 3; I. 780; J. Mr. Kelly paid $74 more.

Week 15, Day 1 (page 73)

A. 12; B. 90, 180, 270, 360; C. 865; D. ounces; E. 2 x 3, 4 x 4, 6 x 2, 2 x 8, 8 x 3, 6 x 3, 6 x 4, 2 x 7, 4 x 5, 6 x 5, 2 x 10 F. 35, 6, 25, 7; G. Check students' work. H. 4; I. 4, 8, 12; J. 30

Week 15, Day 2 (page 74)

A. 4, 9, 36; B. 5:46, 5:31, 6:01; C. 4, 12, 3, 2, 12, 2; D. 12, 3, 12, 12, 6, 6; E. 46; F. 633; G. 15; H. 3, 4; I. 345, 365, 375; J. 8

Week 15, Day 3 (page 75)

A. 4:20 pm; B. $\frac{4}{6}$; C. from top row, left to right: 14, 16, 18, 20, 21, 24, 27, 30, 28, 32, 36, 40, 35, 40, 45, 50; D. 7; E. 12 ÷ 6, 4 ÷ 2, 10 ÷ 5, 12 ÷ 6, 16 ÷ 8, 14 ÷ 7; F. 8, 9, 4, 4, 5, 3; G. Check students' work. H. 24; I.186

Week 15, Day 4 (page 76)

A. 6; B. 28; C. 4; D. 4 $\frac{1}{2}$; E. Check students' work. F. 32; G. 1; H. 5, 3, 6, 2, 5, 4, 4; I. 972; J. 24

Week 16, Day 1 (page 77)

A. 760 + 120; B. 7; C. 5; D. quarter till 9; E. 15 ÷ 5, 15 ÷ 3, 24 ÷ 8, 25 ÷ 5, 27 ÷ 3, 9 ÷ 3, 30 ÷ 6, 81 ÷ 9, 36 ÷ 4, 12 ÷ 4; F. 5, 6, 30; G. Check students' work. H. 7; I. 28, 4, 7; J. 6, Check students' work.

Week 16, Day 2 (page 78)

A. 16, 4, 4; B. 5:40; C. 8, 24, 14, 40, 12, 27, 42, 36; D. 2, 4, 4, 8, 3, 3, 6, 6; E. 492; F. 152; G. 2 ÷ 2 = 1, 10 ÷ 5 = 2,

Answer Key

12 ÷ 6 = 2, 6 ÷ 2 = 3, 12 ÷ 2 = 6,
12 ÷ 2 = 6, 12 ÷ 3 = 4; H. $1; I. 9; J. 8

Week 16, Day 3 (page 79)
A. 18, 3, 6; B. 2 hours 16 minutes;
C. Favorite Ice Cream, vanilla, 2 more;
D. 198; E. 48; F. Vance has 4 mL more;
G. 4, 8, 32; H. >; I. false

Week 16, Day 4 (page 80)
A. 160; B. 8, picture show 32 broken into
4 groups of 8; C. 9; D. 28; E. 22; F. 7;
G. 40, 80, 120; H. 5, 24, 6, 20, 8, 16, 6,
12; I. 703; J. 11:05 am

Week 17, Day 1 (page 81)
A. 5, 7, 35; B. 6; C. 2; D. disagree, A stop
sign is an octagon. E. $5\frac{1}{4}$; F. Yes, she read
706 pages. G. 42, 7, 42, 6; H. 182;
I. intersecting lines; J. 9 hours and 45
minutes

Week 17, Day 2 (page 82)
A. 711; B. 11; C. 0, 6, 12, 5, 0, 10, 0; D. 6,
18, 16, 24, 12, 18, 24; E. 889; F. 160, 180,
160; G. 35, Check students' work. H. 18;
I. 124, 144, 154; J. 7:30 pm

Week 17, Day 3 (page 83)
A. 24, 4, 6; B. $\frac{7}{9}$; C. 6:18, 7:28 5:08;
D. 8; E. 12; F. 6, 3, 4, 7, 2, 4, 2; G. true;
H. grams; I. 7

Week 17, Day 4 (page 84)
A. less than one liter; B. 12, 18, 24; C. 24,
30; D. $17; E. 36, 7, 24, 8; F. 8; G. 28, 7;
H. 6, 3, 1, 4, 8, 7, 9; I. 189; J. Check
students' work.

Week 18, Day 1 (page 85)
A. 7, 8, 56; B. L; C. 5; D. 60; E. 6 x 2,
1 x 2, 4 x 8, 6 x 7, 9 x 8, 2 x 6, 4 x 3
F. 5:00 pm; G. 6; H. 7; I. Check students'
work. J. 42

Week 18, Day 2 (page 86)
A. 18; B. 16; C. 48, 42, 36, 30, 24, 18, 12,
6; D. 9, 8, 7, 6, 5, 4, 3, 2, 1; E. 415; F. 7;
G. 12 ÷ 1, 6 x 2, 3 x 4, 12 x 1, 2 x 6;
H. 18; I. 1; J. 6, 6, 18 ÷ 3 = 6

Week 18, Day 3 (page 87)
A. 9:35; B. 3; C. 3:05 pm; D. 900; E.
about 100; F. 5, 3, 6, 9, 7, 8, 4; G. Check
students' work. H. 16, 4, 4; I. kilograms

Week 18, Day 4 (page 88)
A. 40, 5, 8; B. 4, 16 ÷ 4 = 4; C. 3, 9, 27;
D. 979; E. $\frac{10}{12}$; F. 9; G. false; H. 42; I. 250,
200, 150, 100; J. 16

Week 19, Day 1 (page 89)
A. 3, 8, 24; B. 5, 25, 5; C. 452; D. 4;
E. 12, 15, 12, 18, 30, 24, 16, 20; F. 5, 5,
pentagon; G. 5; H. 993; I. 9, 6, or 6, 9;
J. 24, Check students' work.

Week 19, Day 2 (page 90)
A. 200; B. 8, 12, 4; C. 4; D. 5; E. 6; F. 16;
G. Myra, 3, Kim, Myra, and Bill; H. 3, 7, 21;
I. 622, 612, 592; J. 8

Week 19, Day 3 (page 91)
A. 40, 5, 8; B. 6; C. 2 hours 5 minutes; D. 4;
E. 9; F. 18, 30, 42, 48, 36, 54; G. 4, 9, 36;
H. 511; I. 6

Week 19, Day 4 (page 92)
A. 11:48 am; B. 8; C. true; D. >; E. 42, 56,
48, 35, 49, 64, 30; F. 9; G. 54, 9, 6;
H. 8:00 am; I. 5; J. 10 L

Week 20, Day 1 (page 93)
A. 2, 5, 10, 10, 2, 5; B. 660, 700; C. 667;
D. 11; E. 5, 6, 7, 4, 8, 6, 6, 4, 7, 5, 7; F. 4,
2, 8; G. 9, 6, 9, 54; H. 8; I. 32; J. 8, student
story should describe 64 being divided evenly
into 8 groups of 8

Answer Key

Week 20, Day 2 (page 94)
A. 2 × 3 = 3 × 2; B. Check students' work.
C. 8, 6, 3, 4, 7, 9, 2, 10; D. 24, 32, 16, 40,
0, 36, 20, 28; E. 8; F. 24; G. 12:05 pm;
H. 4, 4, 4, 12; I. 960, 920; J. 3

Week 20, Day 3 (page 95)
A. 24 ft.; B. 4, Check students' work. C. 18;
D. 4; E. 12, 18, 24; F. 12:40 pm; G. 6, 6,
36; H. Check students' work. I. 28, 4, 7

Week 20, Day 4 (page 96)
A. 64 ÷ 8; B. =; C. 8; D. 32; E. 25; F. 56;
G. 7; H. 16; I. 42, 42, 42, 42; J. kilograms

Week 21, Day 1 (page 97)
A. 3, 8, 24; B.14; C. true; D. ÷ 5; E. 0, 9,
18, 27, 36, 45, 54, 63, 72, 81, 90;
F. 11:53; G. 36; H. 6; I. 38; J. 18 ÷ 3 = 6,
Check students' work.

Week 21, Day 2 (page 98)
A. 6, 9, 54; B. from top to bottom, L to R: 4,
8, 12, 16, 20, 8, 16, 24, 32, 40, 12, 24,
36, 48, 60, 16, 32, 48, 64, 80, 20, 40, 60,
80, 100; C. 6, 8, 5, 3,1, 4, 0, 2; D. 24, 21,
45, 49, 48, 0, 42, 28; E. 90, 150, 180;
F. 900; G. 8:15 pm; H. 4; I. 3, 5; J. 28

Week 21, Day 3 (page 99)
A. 2 hours 13 minutes; B. 54, 6, 9;
C. Manuel is incorrect because his fraction
does not show equal-sized pieces. D. 170;
E. 64; F. 9, 9, 7, 8, 8, 9, 7; G. $\frac{3}{8}$, $\frac{4}{8}$; H. 24;
I. 8

Week 21, Day 4 (page 100)
A. 6; B. 36; C. 12; D. 50, 5; E. 2:12, 2:54;
F. 9; G. 9; H. 3$\frac{1}{4}$; I. L; J. =

Week 22, Day 1 (page 101)
A. 6; B. 9; C. 203; D. 5:37 pm; E. 15 ÷ 3,
20 ÷ 4, 25 ÷ 5, 35 ÷ 7, 45 ÷ 9, 10 ÷ 2,

40 ÷ 8, 30 ÷ 6, 50 ÷ 10; F. Check students'
work. G. hexagon; H. 9; I. 8, 16, 2, 8;
J. 5 × 8 = 40, 40 ÷ 5 = 8

Week 22, Day 2 (page 102)
A. 150 + 130; B. 42, Check students' work.
C. 18, 16, 24, 30, 36, 20, 15, 48; D. 8, 2,
3, 8, 6, 6, 8, 6; E. 80, 120, 180; F. 8;
G. 25, 40, 30, 35; H. 26; I. 5, 6; J. 28

Week 22, Day 3 (page 103)
A. 4 × 6 = 24; B. 8, 3, 24; C. 4, 5, 20; D. 6;
E. 40 ÷ 8 = 5; F. 4, 8, 7, 6, 9, 7, 8; G. 35,
Check students' work. H. true; I. 42, 6, 7

Week 22, Day 4 (page 104)
A. 10; B. 21; C. 9; D. 6, 3, 18; E. 5:33 pm;
F. 54; G. 760; H. 32; I. kilograms; J. 7

Week 23, Day 1 (page 105)
A. 7, 7 in each square; B. 18; C. 612; D. 4;
E. 2, 2, 2, 2, 10 ÷ 2 = 5; F.10:49 am; G. 24;
H. 59; I. 7; J. 5:15, 6:00, 4:30

Week 23, Day 2 (page 106)
A. 4 × 5; B. $9; C. 4, 4, 3, 6, 8, 5, 5; D. 42,
0, 21, 30, 24, 32, 20; E. 240, 300, 210;
F. 843; G. 30, 6, 5; H. 28, Check students'
work. I. 523, 543; J. 8

Week 23, Day 3 (page 107)
A. 9, Check students' work. B. 9; C. 7, 28, 7,
28, 28, 7; D. 3; E. 8; F. 8, 8, 9, 3, 9, 9;
G. 2, 6, 4; H. true; I. 6, 9, 6

Week 23, Day 4 (page 108)
A. 40, 5, 8; B. 20; C. true; D. 2; E. 30; F. 7;
G. 160, 480, 640; H. 5$\frac{1}{2}$; I. 118; J. $23

Week 24, Day 1 (page 109)
A. 18, 6; B. 63, 9, 7; C. 4; D. 8; E. 24; F. =;
G. 54; H. 7; I. 250, 420, 320; J. 9:41

Answer Key

Week 24, Day 2 (page 110)
A. 430; B. 16, 32, 48, 64, 80; C. milliliter, liter; D. about 6 g, about 60 kg; E. 339; F. 411; G. blue: 6 × 7, 8 × 4, 3 × 4, 8 × 9, yellow: 7 × 2, 6 × 9, 8 × 8, 8 × 3; H. 2, 4, 6, 20; I. 21, 35; J. 7, 28, 4, 7

Week 24, Day 3 (page 111)
A. 35, array should show 5 rows of 7; B. 15; C. clockwise from 20: 60, 70, 90, 30, 0, 80, 50, 100, 40; D. 6; E. shade in 7 pieces; F. 4, 8, 7, 9, 10, 6; G. Check students' work. H. 745; I. 8

Week 24, Day 4 (page 112)
A. 5, 4, 20; B. 20; C. 9; D. $3\frac{1}{4}$; E. 2:22 pm; F. 8; G. 49; H. 32; I. 20; J. Check students' work.

Week 25, Day 1 (page 113)
A. 1,640, 1,600; B. 40; C. false; D. 18, 21, 42, 28, 48, 24, 56; E. 40; F. 12, Check students' work. G. 2; H. 48; I. 5 kg; J. Check students' work.

Week 25, Day 2 (page 114)
A. $23; B. 5, 3, 15; C. Check students' work. D. Check students' work. E. 8, 48; F. 7, 35; G. 6:35; H. 44; I. 16, 32, 48; J. 32, 4, 8

Week 25, Day 3 (page 115)
A. 32, 4, 8; B. 16; C. 10:52; D. 72, 72, 8; E. 9, drawing should show 18 broken into 2 groups of 9; F. 12, 18, 16, 12, 24, 30, 15; G. >; H. 4, 32; I. 5, 5, 5

Week 25, Day 4 (page 116)
A. 42, Check students' work. B. 27; C. 35, 5, 7; D. 4 triangles, Check students' work. E. 10; F. 6; G. 6; H. 120, 180, 90, 240, 210, 270, 60, 150, 30; I. 12; J. 20

Week 26, Day 1 (page 117)
A. 6:15 pm; B. 3; C. 42, 42; D. 28; E. 24; F. 35; G. 4; H. 3; I. 20; J. 4

Week 26, Day 2 (page 118)
A. 63; B. 24 ÷ 4 = 6, 15 ÷ 3 = 5, 8 ÷ 4 = 2, 15 ÷ 5 = 3, 24 ÷ 3 = 8, 6 ÷ 3 = 2, 12 ÷ 3 = 4; C. 9, 4, 36; D. 6, 4, 3, 2, 7, 1, 5; E. 9; F. 8; G. 2 × 2, 1 × 4, 16 ÷ 4, 20 ÷ 5; H. 3; I. 24, 30, 36; J. 21

Week 26, Day 3 (page 119)
A. 24, 4, 6; B. 18; C. 7:25 pm; D. 859; E. 44 cubes; F. 48; G. Check students' work. H. true; I. 116

Week 26, Day 4 (page 120)
A. 880; B. trapezoid, Check students' work. C. 9; D. 11:35 am; E. $\frac{5}{8}$, $\frac{3}{8}$; F. 54; G. 9; H. 1, 3, 8, 2, 4, 3, 9, 10; I. Check students' work. J. 12

Week 27, Day 1 (page 121)
A. $\frac{11}{16}$; B. 4 in.; C. 76; D. about 60; E. 6, 9; F. 5, 9, 45; G. 80; H. 4; I. 8; J. strawberries, bananas, 1

Week 27, Day 2 (page 122)
A. 6, 3, 2; B. 3:19; C. 28, 21, 42, 0, 14, 63, 7, 70, 56; D. 8, 2, 6, 5, 1, 2, 10, 9, 3; E. 4, 28; F. milliliters; G. top to bottom, L to R: 16, 24, 40, 24, 36, 60, 40, 60, 100; H. 29; I. 695, 725, 755; J. 565

Week 27, Day 3 (page 123)
A. 6, 7, 42; B. about 10; C. yellow: 5 ÷ 5, 30 ÷ 6, 6 ÷ 2, blue: 24 ÷ 6, 32 ÷ 4; D. 277; E. 12; F. 36, 35, 0, 24, 54, 42, 40; G. Point Y; H. $22; I. 8

Week 27, Day 4 (page 124)
A. 1:28 pm; B. 19; C. 49; D.19; E. 48; F. 2; G. 71; H. 24 ÷ 6, 12 Ð 8, 2 × 2, 12 ÷ 3, 4 × 1, 40 ÷ 10, 6 Ð 2, 32 ÷ 8, 8 Ð 4; I. 3; J. <

Answer Key

Week 28, Day 1 (page 125)
A. $\frac{7}{9}$; B. 460, 230, 230; C. true; D. less than one liter; E. 40; F. 36, 6, 6; G. 7:26; H. 702; I. 9, 54, 9, 6; J. The 5:45 pm number line should show 3 one hour hops to 5:30 and one 15 minute hop to 5:45.

Week 28, Day 2 (page 126)
A. $12; B. 1:30 pm; C. 6, 8, 9, 9, 4, 5, 7, 7; D. 6, 7, 28, 4, 8, 24; E. 16; F. 3; G. 6, Check students' work. H. 16; I. 36, 45, 54, 63, 72; J. 4, 9, 36

Week 28, Day 3 (page 127)
A. <; B. 3; C. 48 cupcakes; D. 100; E. 7; F. 6 × 2, 3 × 5, 3 × 6, 4 × 3, 4 × 6; G. 6 $\frac{1}{2}$; H. 21, 3, 7; I. 9

Week 28, Day 4 (page 128)
A. $\frac{4}{5} = \frac{8}{10}$; B. 4, 7, 28; C. 9; D. 6, 6 ; E. 9; F. 8; G. 102; H. pentagon; I. 810; J. Check students' work.

Week 29, Day 1 (page 129)
A. $\frac{2}{8}$, $\frac{6}{8}$; B. 28; C. 8,8; D. 17; E. rhombus, quadrilateral, parallelogram; F. 24; G. true; H. 7; I. 8; J. 11

Week 29, Day 2 (page 130)
A. 32, 4, 8; B. Check students' work. C. 4, 8, 2, 12, 5, 6; D. 2, 5, 6, 3, 8, 4; E. 943; F. 420, 560, 720; G. 7:50; H. 200, 400, 600; I. 585, 570; J. <

Week 29, Day 3 (page 131)
A. 8, Check students' work. B. 4, 6, 24; C. >; D. 5; E. $7; F. 63, 42, 56, 48, 72, 49, 54; G. 8 $\frac{3}{4}$; H. 6; I. 6

Week 29, Day 4 (page 132)
A. perpendicular lines; B. >; C. true; D. 7:43; E. Check students' work. F. 9; G. 5; H. 54 ÷ 6, 81 ÷ 9, 56 ÷ 8, 49 ÷ 7, 30 ÷ 6, 15 ÷ 3,

27 ÷ 9, 12 ÷ 4, 25 ÷ 5, 6 ÷ 6; I. 828; J. $\frac{4}{6}$

Week 30, Day 1 (page 133)
A. 4:35; B. Check students' work. C. 2; D. 40; E. 27; F. 32+16=48; G. grams; H. 6; I. 9; J. Check students' work.

Week 30, Day 2 (page 134)
A. 2 hours, 30 minutes; B. 7; C. 36, 40, 0, 28, 42, 56; D. 7, 9, 4, 9, 6, 8; E. 16; F. 4; G. <; H. 4, 8, 4; I. true; J. $\frac{2}{8}$, $\frac{4}{8}$, $\frac{6}{8}$

Week 30, Day 3 (page 135)
A. <; B. 4; C. 6, 7, 42, 42, 6, 7; D. 837; E. =; F. 6, 12, 18, 24; G. 8; H. 8; I. 7

Week 30, Day 4 (page 136)
A. 16, 16, 48, 48, 96; B. 6:40 pm; C. 7, 42, 6, 7; D. $\frac{4}{6} > \frac{4}{12}$; E. 12; F. 325; G. 9; H. 56, 54, 72, 48, 42, 0, 32, 49; I. mL; J. Check students' work.

Week 31, Day 1 (page 137)
A. >; B. 8; C. 56, 56; D. $\frac{2}{5}$; E. 30; F. 1:03 pm; G. 9, 27, 3, 9; H. 124; I. 400, 200; J. Check students' work.

Week 31, Day 2 (page 138)
A. 21, 3, 7; B. 48 ÷ 8 = 6, 32 ÷ 4 = 8, 27 ÷ 9 = 3, 28 ÷ 4 = 7, 24 ÷ 8 = 3, 48 ÷ 6 = 8; C. 21, 35, 56, 28, 49, 63; D. 8, 5, 7, 1, 4, 10; E. Check students' work. F. Check students' work. G. Check students' work. H. >; I. 32, 40, 48; J. 9

Week 31, Day 3 (page 139)
A. $\frac{3}{5} > \frac{2}{10}$; B. 9 hours and 40 minutes; C. 9, 9, 3; D. 732; E. Check students' work. F. 24, 32, 40, 48, 56, 64; G. 6 markers; H. 26; I. kilograms

Week 31, Day 4 (page 140)
A. 430180; B. Check students' work. C. 63, 63; D. 8, 8, 32, 32, 64; E. line segment AB;

Answer Key

F. 8; G. Check students' work. H. 48, 8, 42, 6, 64, 8, 56, 8; I. $\frac{4}{16}$; J. 6

Week 32, Day 1 (page 141)

A. 24; B. Check students' work. C. 45, 45; D. >; E. 20, 0, 18, 28, 24, 0, 10, 36, 42, 40; F. 5:42; G. 8; H. 590; I. 6 cm; J. Check students' work.

Week 32, Day 2 (page 142)

A. 32 slices; B. 26; C. 6, 10, 3, 5, 8; D. 2, 3, 4, 5, 1; E. 28; F. 1; G. yellow: 8 x 8, 6 x 6, 4 x 4, green: 7 x 7, 9 x 9, 5 x 5; H. 6; I. 350, 375, 425; J. 2:35 pm

Week 32, Day 3 (page 143)

A. Each point should be evenly spaced: 0, $\frac{1}{8}$, $\frac{2}{8}$, $\frac{3}{8}$, $\frac{4}{8}$, $\frac{5}{8}$, $\frac{6}{8}$, $\frac{7}{8}$, 1. B.16; C. >; D. 6; E. 8; F. 5, 8, 4, 9, 6, 3, 2; G. 4:43; H. 6; I. kilograms

Week 32, Day 4 (page 144)

A. 21; B. 9; C. <; D. No, a pot of soup would probably only hold about 2 or 3 liters; E. 12, 24, 36, 48, 60; F. 72; G. 8; H. quadrilateral, rectangle, parallelogram; I. 864; J. Check students' work.

Week 33, Day 1 (page 145)

A. Check students' work. B. 6; C. 222; D. 20, 5, 4; E. $5\frac{1}{4}$; F. 1:49 pm; G. 9; H. 42; I. 360, 450, 540; J. Check students' work.

Week 33, Day 2 (page 146)

A. 45; B. Check students' work. C. 28, 3, 42, 5, 14, 7; D. 4, 8, 8, 20, 7, 12; E. 3; F. 42; G. 32, 4, 8; H. 21; I. 351, 431; J. 4

Week 33, Day 3 (page 147)

A. 10:32 pm; B. Kent had 17 mL more. C. $\frac{1}{6}$, $\frac{2}{12}$; D. 9; E. 3 dollars; F. 6, 4, 32, 36, 10, 5; G.16; H. false; I. Check students' work.

Week 33, Day 4 (page 148)

A. trapezoid; B. $\frac{3}{5} < \frac{7}{10}$; C. true; D. July, August, 3; E. 4 bottles; F. 56; G. 9; H. 36 ÷ 6, 40 ÷ 5 56 ÷ 7, 18 ÷ 3, 48 ÷ 6, 32 ÷ 8, 16 ÷ 4, 24 ÷ 3, 64 ÷ 8, 20 ÷ 10; I. grams; J. $\frac{10}{12}$

Week 34, Day 1 (page 149)

A. 4, 6, 24; B. 420, 720, 300, 450; C. 146; D. 6; E. 6, 4, 6, 7, 4, 4, 8, 6; F. 3:16 pm; G. 2; H. 7; I. false; J. 4, Check students' work.

Week 34, Day 2 (page 150)

A. 8; B. 32; C. 24, 21, 32, 48, 28, 42, 18; D. 9, 3, 4, 8, 6, 9, 4; E. Top to bottom, L to R: 2, 1, 4; F. Top to bottom, L to R: 8, 3, 4; G. 35, 5, 7; H. 24; I. 552, 577, 602; J. <

Week 34, Day 3 (page 151)

A. =; B. 18; C. 9:40 pm; D. 4; E. 30, 6, 5, 6, 5, 30; F. 5, 7, 8, 3, 5, 8; G. $6\frac{3}{4}$; H. $40; I. 48

Week 34, Day 4 (page 152)

A. ray; B. 3; C. true; D. <; E. 43; F. 4; G. 6; H. 24, 35, 42, 21, 32, 48, 0, 7; I. 717; J. 25 mL

Week 35, Day 1 (page 153)

A. student should draw two lines that meet to form a right angle; B. $\frac{9}{12}$; C. 60, 10; D. 42, 54, 40, 45, 49, 48, 36, 56; E. 6; F. 9:43; G. 9; H. 8; I. 753; J. student should write to describe 28 broken into 7 groups of 4

Week 35, Day 2 (page 154)

A. <; B. $41; C. 32, 56, 64, 48, 0, 80; D. 4, 6, 1, 3, 7, 8; E. 9; F. Top to bottom, L to R: 8, 6, 3; G. 32; H. 35, 5, 7; I. 286, 271, 256; J. 6, 8, 48

Answer Key

Week 35, Day 3 (page 155)
A. $\frac{8}{8}$, 1; B. Check students' work. C. 2:39, 1:34, 3:44; D. 6; E.14; F. 5, 12, 2, 3, 8, 9; G. $\frac{1}{3}$, $\frac{2}{3}$; H. 4, 4; I. >

Week 35, Day 4 (page 156)
A. acute angle; B. 12; C. 42; D. 8, Check students' work. E. 4:10 pm; F. 9; G. 155; H. <; I. $\frac{8}{10}$; J. 72

Week 36, Day 1 (page 157)
A. >; B. 2 hours, 11min; C. 56, 56; D. 7; E. $3\frac{1}{4}$; F. 10, 16; G. 4; H. 2; I. 7; J. Check students' work.

Week 36, Day 2 (page 158)
A. <; B. Check students' work. 42 ÷ 6 = 7; C. 12, 24, 28, 8, 4, 20; D. 18, 15, 12, 24, 0, 27; E. 364; F. 214; G. 28; H. 48; I.18, 45, 54; J. 8, 80, 16, 96

Week 36, Day 3 (page 159)
A. 22 minutes to 7; B. Check students' work.; C. Check students' work. D. 764; E. 3, 6, 18; F. 8, 10, 12, 14, 16; G. Points on the number line should be labeled $\frac{1}{8}$, $\frac{2}{8}$, $\frac{3}{8}$, $\frac{4}{8}$ at the same points of $\frac{1}{2}$, $\frac{5}{8}$, $\frac{6}{8}$, and $\frac{7}{8}$. H. 510, 380, 130; I. true

Week 36, Day 4 (page 160)
A. Check students' work. B. 10, 60, 36, 96; C.12:20 pm; D. 40, Check students' work. E. 48, 28; F. 6; G. 72; H. × 3, × 5, × 4, × 4, × 4, × 3, × 3; I. 534; J. student should trace the perpendicular lines that form the right angle of the triangle

Week 37, Day 1 (page 161)
A. 2 hours 20 minutes; B. 8; C. 30; D. 9; E. $7\frac{1}{2}$; F. 23, 24; G. shade 4 out of 10 parts; H. 9; I. 9; J. yellow, pink, 16, 12

Week 37, Day 2 (page 162)
A. 490 – 210; B. 48, 6, 8; C. 4, 5, 8, 10, 9, 1, 3; D. 6, 32, 16, 12, 18, 24, 36; E. less than 1 L; F. about 1 g; G. 7, Check students' work. H. >; I. 485, 470, 455; J. 18

Week 37, Day 3 (page 163)
A. 4, 8, 32; B. 7, 28, 56; C. blue: 4 × 2, 6 × 8, 4 × 8, yellow: 9 × 3, 7 × 3, 3 × 5; D. 7, 7; E. $12; F. 9, 8, 7, 5, 6; G. Check students' work. H. 6; I.10

Week 37, Day 4 (page 164)
A. pentagon; B. 30, 6, 5; C. 6, 48, 48, 96; D. <; E. 14, 22; F. 6; G. 8; H. 36 ÷ 9, 12 ÷ 3, 16 ÷ 2, 16 ÷ 4, 20 ÷ 5, 24 ÷ 6, 42 ÷ 7, 28 ÷ 7, 8 ÷ 4; I. 634; J. 48

Week 38, Day 1 (page 165)
A. 18, 6, 3; B. $\frac{10}{12}$; C. 9, 9; D. 21, 20; E. $8\frac{1}{2}$; F. 6:35 pm; G. 10; H. 8; I. Check students' work. J. 8, 4, 32, 32, 8, 4

Week 38, Day 2 (page 166)
A. $\frac{7}{12}$; B. 10, 18; C. 21, 32, 42, 40, 54, 24, 30; D. 6, 8, 8, 6, 9, 9, 7; E. 18; F. 996; G. 8, Check students' work. H. 6; I. 4, 8; J. >

Week 38, Day 3 (page 167)
A. >; B. 9 cm; C. 32 ÷ 4 = 8, Check students' work. D. 8; E. parallelogram or rhombus; F. 36, 12, 42, 48, 54, 0; G. Check students' work. H. 12, 12, 24; I. 9

Week 38, Day 4 (page 168)
A. 63 ÷ 7; B. 8, 8, 8; C. 18; D. 42, 6, 7; E. 28; F. 5; G. 32; H. × 7, × 4, × 3, × 5, × 4, × 7; I. 10; J. =

Week 39, Day 1 (page 169)
A. more than 1 liter; B. $18; C. 7, 8; D. 30 feet; E. 8, 6, 4, 8, 8, 8, 2, 5, 4; F. 1:35 pm; G. Check students' work. H. 733; I. 63, 7, 9; J. Check students' work.

Answer Key

Week 39, Day 2 (page 170)
A. $\frac{2}{8}$, or $\frac{1}{4}$; B. 5, 42; C. 4, 4, 4, 7, 7, 4, 7;
D. 42, 24, 25, 32, 24, 56, 36; E. >; F. 4;
G. $\frac{2}{3} < \frac{3}{4}$; H. 40; I. 54, 45, 27; J. 24

Week 39, Day 3 (page 171)
A. =; B. 63, 9, 7; C. 8, 6, 48; D. 48, 8, 6;
E. 2; F. Check students' work. G. 5, 18, 9,
12, 10; H. Check students' work. I. 36;
J. 252

Week 39, Day 4 (page 172)
A. $\frac{3}{5}$; B. Check students' work. C. 3, 50, 15,
65; D. 16, 12, 16+12= 28, 28; E. >; F. 8;
G. split into 3 equal parts; H. 6 $\frac{3}{4}$; I. 48;
 J. 9:57 pm

Week 40, Day 1 (page 173)
A. $\frac{3}{4} = \frac{9}{12}$; B. Mya; C. false; D. 6 hours 45
minutes; E. 30, 3, 10; F. 56, Check students'
work. G. Check students' work. H. 26; I. 28
mL; J. Check students' work.

Week 40, Day 2 (page 174)
A. Check students' work. B. 8:22, 5:07; C.
18, 24, 28, 30, 48, 36, 27; D. 9, 8, 4, 5, 5,
6, 6; E. 2; F. 5; G. Check students' work.
H. 22; I. $\frac{9}{3}$, 3; J. 1 hour and 45 minutes

Week 40, Day 3 (page 175)
A. 760; B. 9; C. 21+30= 51, 51; D. 182;
E. 6; F. 7, 24, 3, 20, 8; G. 10:55 am, Check
students' work. H. 18; I. 2

Week 40, Day 4 (page 176)
A. line segment; B. $\frac{1}{3} < \frac{6}{9}$; C. 7, 4, 140, 28,
168; D. 3 in.; E. 13, 18; F. 10; G. >;
H. 63÷7, 42÷6, 28÷4, 21÷7, 15÷5, 20÷4,
8÷8, 54÷6; I. more than 1 gram; J. 5, 15